Resurrection, Sex and God

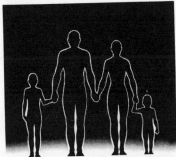

Essays on the Foundations of Faith

by
Arthur Frederick Ide
John R. Rogers
Joseph S. Zemel

Arthur Frederick Ide, Editor

Dallas
Minuteman
1990

© 1990, Minuteman Press

Library of Congress Cataloging-in-Publication Data

Resurrection, sex, and God : essays on the foundations of faith /
   by Arthur Frederick Ide, John R. Rogers, Joseph S. Zemel :
   Arthur Frederick Ide, editor.
            p.   cm.
   Contents: An examination of the biblical evidence for the
resurrection of Jesus / by John R. Rogers - - On the non-
existence of God / by Joseph S. Zemel - - The physical Jesus /
by Arthur Frederick Ide.
   Includes bibliographical references.
   ISBN 0-926899-01-5 : $10.00
   1. Jesus Christ - - Resurrection.   2. God -- Proof. 3. Jesus
Christ -- Sexual behavior.   I. Ide, Arthur Frederick.
II. Rogers, John R. (John Raymond), 1946 -   .
III. Zemel, Joseph S., 1965 -   .
BT481.R455   1990   90-33786
232.9 - - dc20   CIP

For

Freda Kernes
Philadelphia, Pennsylvania

Sheila Ogea and Henry Schmuck
Detroit, Michigan

Stephen and Julie Thorne
Escondido, California

and to the thousands who seek
fact not fiction
reason not emotion
substance not style
reality not fantasy
and aren't afraid to read
to debate
to question
and hold fast to the First Amendment
the separation of state and church
the right to publish and disagree.

Table of Contents

6

Introduction

The Jesus of contemporary Christianity is sterile. Emasculated and sanitized, this twentieth century god is protected by screaming multitudes who two thousand years ago would have demanded his crucifixion, if indeed he had been a man and had walked the dusty roads of Galilee. More close to the plastic statues that ride the dash-boards of modern cars than the sweat-stained and odor-riddled mortals that fought for their very existence two thousand years ago, the Jesus that thousands worship today would not have been recognized by his disciples yesterday, if, in fact, they too had existed.

The essays contained in this volume address the physical questions concerning this man from Nazareth. They look at physical realities and judge whether or not contemporary hagiography is justified or realistic. The intent of each essayist is to unsettle, to provoke thought and debate, and to come to a more realistic understanding and appreciation of the legends and lore that have grown up around an alleged mortal who, it is believed by many, taught a kinder and more gentle ethic than the barbaric hatred the permeated Jewish society in the first one hundred years of the contemporary era (CE). To do this, each essayist has pruned away "miracles," for "miracles" aren't substantiated by other records. Miracles, instead, take from the fantasies of other ontologies current in the days of the Caesars before Nero burned Rome.

While this gathering of papers doesn't address such questions as whether or not Jesus existed, nor the reality of or proof for miracles, the authors of the individual offerings do argue that (1) Jesus was sexual, and probably gay; (2) that the alleged resurrection was at best a part of an initiation rite, and (3) the concept of god existing has been fashioned by men for men who feared logic and reason. The primary source, in each essay, are the gospels. They are supplemented by other contemporary records. Where it's essential, the original is given in the text; otherwise, where necessary, it's printed in the end notes. Each author is responsible for his own work. The editor accepts general responsibility for the collection.

Since the essayists depend heavily on the gospels, it's sound to spend a moment and discuss their origin and development. The four "recognized" (authentic or canonized) gospels are those considered to be by Matthew, Mark, Luke and John.

Mark is considered to be the oldest gospel. It is in Mark that we read how Jesus selected the men he would keep near him for the last three years of his life.

The author of Mark wants the reader to believe that Jesus didn't know his disciples before spotting them either fishing in the Sea of Galilee, or in their boats, mending nets (Mark 1:16-20). Once the men were selected, allegedly by divine inspiration, Jesus cures the mad—"casting out demons" from those possessed (1.28). For this "miracle" he immediately attracted a large crowd that followed him (1: 32-45f). But while he "saved others, he cannot save himself." (15.31).

Mark, written probably in 75 CE, is the foundation for both the gospels according to Matthew and Luke. Both Matthew and Luke use other, earlier, sources, but these sources have been lost or destroyed. What has been preserved is the alleged statements made by Jesus. They too are miracle stories (Matt. 12:22f, 21:14f, Luke 4.16-30, 5:1-11 and 7: 16f, 9:43). Each time a miracle is performed, Jesus' retinue is increased.

John is the only gospel that claims the miracles are proof Jesus had supernatural status (1:48-50f; 2:11, 23f; 3:2). They are reported so that "you may believe that Jesus is the Messiah, the Son of God."   (20:30f).

When the gospels are considered as a whole, approached and read as records of happenings and not theological tracts trading on faith, we learn several interesting points that modern theologians overlook:

- Jesus was a man.
- Jesus was a magician (performer of feats/miracles).
- Jesus wanted recognition.
- Because he peformed miracles some thought he was a "god."

No one can discount the significance of Jesus as a miracle worker. Throughout early Christian communities, Jesus was first, and foremost, hailed as "a worker of miracles"—not as a "savior."[1]

Jesus was also like contemporary evangelists. He needed those he cured to believe in their own cure. And he was upset with those who didn't believe: "He marveled at their unbelief." (και εθαυμεζε δια την απιστιαν αυτων) (Mark 6:6). In light of this it is easily understood why the Jews refused to accept Jesus as the Messiah once he had been crucified: he could not save himself. For this reason the resurrection narrative had to be written so that it would become the ultimate miracle and restore the "faith" of the Jews in the Great Magician (*magi* or rabbi) Jesus. This also fits the facts of psychology. A faith healer can't heal where there's no faith. John R. Rogers, a brilliant and articulate young man who glories in the green lush of West Virginia, easily picks up on this theme, massaging each word until it relaxes under his analysis, and then with a probing tenderness, exposes the raw flesh gnawed by fiction for the world to see.

Once the myth of the resurrection is removed, it's but a small move to expose the concept of god, as Joseph S. Zemel of Philadelphia does with resounding eclat. Once god is not there, all that can be left is man, a person forgotten in quest of an eternal, immovable, remote source that controls the infinitely expanding. Jesus won acclaim as a miracle worker and as a rabble rouser, similar to Thadeus who "arose, saying he was Somebody, and to him some four hundred men attached themselves. He was killed, all who believed in him were scattered and [the movement] came to nothing. After him Judas the Galilean arose in the days of the census and led off [into revolution] the people who followed him, and he perished and all of those who believed in him were scattered. Therefore I say, keep [your hands] off these men and let them go, as if this plan or undertaking is [merely] human, it will go to pieces [too] ..." (προ γαρ τουτων των δμερων ανεστη Θευδας λεγων ειναι τινα εαυτον ω προσεκλιθη ανδρων αριθμος ως τετρακοσιων ος αυηρεθη και παντες οσοι επειθοντο αυτω διελτυθησαν και εγενοντο εις ουδεν· μετα τουτον ανεστη Ιουδας ο Γαλιλαιος εν ταις ημεραις της απογραφης και απεστησε λαον οπισω αυτου κακεινος απωλετθ και παντας οσοι επειθοντο αυτωδιεσκορπισθησαν και ταν λεγω υμιν αποστητε απο των ανθρωπων τουτων και αφετε αυτους οτι εαν η εξ ανθρωπων η βουλη αυτη η το εργον τουτο καταλυθησεται Acts 5:35-38). This passage is to be questioned with care, for the Christians could not have had one of their number within the Sanhedrin to report the dialog. But it's import is apparent: other movements broke up because they were human-led and human-inspired. If their movement was to succeed, then their leader had to be declared a god and their movement divinely-led. It is because of this that the mortality, the humanity, the sexuality of Jesus had to be downplayed and covered. It is for that reason I approached the gospels to dig out the basic nature of a man that only the Christian bible, as a contemporary source, says lived on this planet of earth and water. If he lived he would have had to be sexual and tempted. The fact that his closest allies, his boon companions, and in fact the one that he loved most of all—and allowed this "Beloved" to rest his head upon his own chest—says that Jesus was a homosexual. This behavior was neither common nor was it

11

acceptable nor tolerated. Such actions "belonged to the Greeks." Not to "good and true men of Israel." The disciples had enough problems with what the people thought of Jesus when he was crucified. Some thought he was a Galilean (John 7:41). To be a Galilean was a reproach in Jerusalem which had no time for those from "the north-country"— where their accent kept them in the public eye. Others thought he was a Samaritan possessed by a demon (John 8. 48), the land of Samaria being famous for its magicians (Acts 8:9ff).[2] That such labels were attached to Jesus shows that he wasn't of distinguished ancestry—inspite of the gospel writers effort to present him as being a member of the House of King David. Even some of them admitted, "We don't know where he comes from" (John 9:29).

To be considered a country-bumkin—a man from the north or from Samaria—was considered a curse by itself. But to add homosexuality to this social stigma made the man even less acceptable.

To be known as a homosexual, and a practicing homosexual, would only further hurt the disciples cause. Some were zealots, determined to win Israel's freedom from Rome. They couldn't risk further social ostracization—as the people demanded a king who would be a warrior to lead them out of their current captivity when Jesus rode in on Palm Sunday (John 12:12-16).

The disciples needed the loyalty of as many people as possible, therefore they couldn't rid Jesus of his lover—Lazarus—while he lived. For when Jesus "restored" Lazarus to the living, Lazarus became a visual miracle that people raced to see: 'A great multitude therefore of the Jews knew that he was there, and they came not for Jesus' sake only, but that they might see Lazarus, whom [Jesus] raised from the dead. [For this reason] the chief priests thought to kill Lazarus, also". Εγνω ουν ο οχλος πολυς εκ των Ιουδαιων οτι εκε εστι και ηλθον ου δια του Ιησουν μονον αλλ ινα και τον Λαζαρον ιδωσιν ον ηγειρεν εκ νεκρων· εβουλευσαντο δε οι αρχιερεις ωα και τον Λαζαρον αποκτεινωσιν· (John 12:9-10). The high priests, who were obligated to obey the Laws of Moses, could not tolerate a homosexual to live[3]—especially a man so close to Jesus that the communities through which they passed rejoiced in their love affair: "The Jews, therefore, said, "Behold how he loved him". εδακρυσεν ο Ιησους ελεγον ουν οι Ιουδαιθι Ιδε τως εφιλει αυτον (John 11:36).[4]

Since homosexuality was a crime in Israel, but not in Rome, the early Christians were in a quandry. Jesus had said nothing about it. Nor did any of his immediate disciples.

There were gays and lesbians in the apostleship and discipleship. As Christianity spread in the empire, those who turned to it most readily were the soldiers. Many of these soldiers were gay. Some of them married other gay men in ceremonies during the worship of Mithra—before it was supplanted with the worship of Jesus. Both the Mithra mass and the early Christian *agape* had strong gay overtones.

Homosexuality didn't become an illegal act that was *enforced* until the days of the Emperor Justinian. Then it was enforced only as a way of winning church support for civil legislation. The state adopted the church's stand spawned by sexually suppressed and frustrated men who gained control over the militant arm of the church through their writings. Wanting to rid the world of sex and regeneration, while concentrating on the resurrection of the soul and its entrance into a new world of sexlessness promised by St. Paul (Gal. 3:28), these church "fathers" declared the once-sacred act of love to be a "sin."[5] Yet the record points out clearly that Jesus enjoyed and participated in this very "sin."

—Arthur Frederick Ide

Cedar Falls, Iowa
The Summer Equinox, 1989

NOTES

[1]Mark 5:14, 18, 22, 24, 27; 6:54ff; 7:25, 32; 8:22; 9:17; 10:13, 50f. Note that Jesus even performed "miracles" on the Sabbath (acts which were against the rigid code and laws): Luke 14:5; Matt. 12:11. The writers of the gospels justified this action, claiming prophecy to that effect: Isaiah 53:4; cp. Matt. 8:17 and 11: 28. It was because of the alleged miracles that the writers proclaimed Jesus to be the "messiah": Matt. 11:2-6; 12:15-21; 21:14f. Mark 10:47f; 11:10; 15:31f. Luke 7:18-23. John 1:48f; 4:29; 7:31; 20:30f. What is interesting in this regard is that Jesus had earlier gone to another prophet (John the Baptist) for sanctification, requiring Matt. 3:14f to explain it, and John 1:29-34 to suppress it. For commentary, see: O. Boecher, *Christus Exorcista* (Stuttgart, 1972); 96 *Beitraege zur Wissenschaft vom Alten und Neuen Testament*. See also: G. Stanton, *Jesus of Nazareth in New Testament Preaching* (Cambridge: The University Press,1974); 27 *Studiorum Novi Testamenti Societas*. In most cases, Jesus is chasing out mythological adversaries (such as Satan, demons, and so forth): Mark 1:13, Luke 22:31, John 13:2, 27. to cite a few.

[2]Territory west of the Jordan, bounded by Galilee on the north and Judea on the south, after the death of Herod the Great it was assigned to Archelaus, and ultimately to Syria. On Jewish hostility, see John 4, 9, 8, 48, which is not in keeping with Jesus' parable on the Good Samaritan (Luke 10:33) and the ten lepers (Luke 17:16), further setting him apart from mainstream Judaism. Part of the popular objection to the Samaritans is because as a people they had their own version of the Pentateuch, in Hebrew, and it only accepts a part of the Old Testament, which they received from the Jews at the time of Nehemiah (Neh. 13:23-31). A 13th century manuscript is preserved in the Vatican Library.

[3]Leviticus 18:22, the reasoning behind the law is because homosexuality, at that time, was (1) a part of pagan worship services, and (2) thought to be non-hygenic (see Leviticus 18:+), and this prohibition (18:22) follows immediately after the prohibition on idolatrous sexuality. It is the religious implication, not the physical act which is condemned (cp. 2 Kings 16:3). This is made more emphatic in the early Greek translations, with $\beta\delta\epsilon\lambda\upsilon\gamma\mu\alpha$ used to show that such an act is considered an infringement on ritual purity, which is read as monotheistic worship.

[4]St. Aelred, abbot of Rievaulx, not only discusses the "perfect love" that Jesus and John had, but likens their relationship to a "marriage. See: Aelred of Rievaulx, *De speculo caritatis*, in Aelred of Rievaulx, *Aelredi Rievallensis opera omnia*, ed. A. Hoste and H. Talbot. Corpus Christianorum. (Turnhout, 1971), III.109-110. The Roman Catholic church and its apologists have worked diligently at striking this "offending" entry from the writings of Aelred.

Aelred was commonly known as the "Bernard of the North," spending some time at the court of King David of Scotland. He is better known as the biographer of St. Edward the Confessor, yet it is his theological writings (which combine mysticism and speculative theology) that won him acclaim in England in his own day and throughout the world today. (See: *Opera Ascetica*, in B. Tissier, *Bibliotheca Patrum Cisterciensium* V (Bono-Fonte, 1662), pp. 162-388; *Opera Historica* in R. Twysden, *Historiae Anglicanae Scriptores Decem* (London, 1652), cols. 337-422; both reprinted in the Latin in J.-P. Migne (ed.), *Patrologia ... Latina* (221 vols. Paris, 1844-1864), CXCV, cols. 209-796. For a quality contemporary (twentieth century) discussion on Aelred's views and impact on the development of gay life and gay theology, see J. Michael Clark, M.Div., Ph.D. (Emory University, Atlanta), *Gay Being, Divine Presence: Essays in Gay Spirituality (The* Ganymede *Papers)* (Garland, TX: Tangelwuld Press, 1987), pp. 48-54.

The reason Aelred had no objection to homosexuality, is because he observed it in animals. This showed him that homosexuality was natural since it occurs in nature. He accepted it as a matter of fact: "Sicut equus et mulus quibus non est intellectus irruit in virum quem feminam ess putabet," in *De sanctimoniali de Wattum* in *Patrologia ... Latina* CXCV col. 793.

Justinian's law did not come into effect until 538 CE. See: Justinian, *Novella* 77:1-2. Punishment, if convicted of the crime, was castration (see: Procopius, *Anecdota* XI:36). Prior to the stranglehold of Christianity on the state, the issue of homosexuality was a private matter (see: Plutarch, *Amatorius*, 749F). For gay marriages among soldiers, see: Martial 1.24, 11.42, and Juvenal 2.117-142. Martial points out that both men were thoroughly masculine: "Barbatus rigido nupsit ...." For a further discussion, see my: *Gomorrah & the Rise of Homophobia* (Las Colinas, TX: The Liberal Press, 1985), and, for an indepth appraisal: John Boswell, *Christianity, Social Tolerance, and Homosexuality; Gay People in Western Europe from the Beginning of the Christian Era to the Fourteenth Century* (Chicago: University of Chicago Press, 1980).

[5]Objections to homosexuality was, for the most part, because the fathers who opposed it were personally disturbed by their own overt or covert homosexuality, as was the case with Chrysostom. Others opposed it because they believed the passion within the act was either addictive or obsessive, while some considered it evil as they heard (or experienced) that one of the partners was passive—a trait considered ungodly in a man. See: Theodoret of Cyrus, *Therapeutique des maladies helleniques* [*Graecarum affectionum curatio*] in *Sources chretiennes* (Paris, 1958), vol. 57, pp. 352-353 (9:53-54). Still, several saints—such as St. Paulinus, bishop of Nola, were passionately and actively gay, regardless of the church's official stand. They found their inspiration in Jesus' love for John/Lazarus.

AN EXAMINATION OF THE BIBLICAL EVIDENCE
FOR THE RESURRECTION OF JESUS[1]

by John R. Rogers

Few historical periods of the ancient world have been well documented. This is especially true in the Age of the reputed Hebrew messiah, Jesus.

No ancient historian has made such a boastful claim that the Nazarene actually lived. All references are to citation of others about the anointed of the desert (*Christus* = Christ, meaning "anointed'). Still, Christians throughout the current era have argued, unsubstantially, that two "historians" (Josepheus, a Pharisee, and Tacitus, a pagan) have given witness to this alleged savior.

Neither Josephus, nor Tacitus, were eyewitnesses to the existence or preaching of Jesus. Flavius Josephus was born around the year 37 and reputedly died in 100 of the current era (CE). In 66 CE, Josephus took a leading part in the Jewish war. In 67 CE, he was taken prisoner by Vespasian, and during the seige of Jerusalem Josephus served as interpreter to Titus, with whom he returned to Rome. His account of the events that surrounded his life is known as *Jewish War*, probably written in Aramaic.[2] It is recognized as an apology to gain sympathy from the Romans, and thus Josephus minimizes the role of the Zealots and the importance of the Messianic hope.

Josephus' second work, *Antiquities of the Jews*,[3] traces the history of the Jews from the "Creation" to the end of the Jewish wars. In it, Josephus incorporates the narratives of Dionysius of Halicarnassus, Nicolaus of Damascus, as well as Apocryphal books. The infamous reference to "Jesus" (18.3.3) calling the "Christ" "a wise man, if indeed one should call him a man," is not authentic.[4] That particular passage was added an expanded on by later Christian writers before the days of the bishop Eusebius, who referenced it in its current form.[5]

Cornelius Tacitus was born 55 CE and died in 120 CE. Little is known about him, although some of his works survive. In his *Annals* 15.44, Tacitus mentions the persecution of the Christians by Nero. He claims that the Christians were made scapegoats to cover Nero's torching of Rome. While he held the Christians guiltless, he believed their religion to be a pernicious superstition (*exitiabilis superstitio*). He does not, in any passage, recognize the existence of a Jesus of Nazareth, much less say that Jesus was a god.[6]

At most Josephus and Tacitus recognized the presence of the sect or cult of Christians. All other secular historians are quiet on this legend of a man of god coming out of Galilee.

The only "authentic" testimony to existence of Jesus, is that written by Saul of Tarsus (St. Paul), and the Gospels (regardless of who was the author of what). Even then, the writtings of Saul date around 47 CE and later — long after the alleged death of Jesus. Saul's ideas were taught twenty to thirty years *before* any of the official gospel writers penned their accounts. Therefore, his letters (*epistles*), and account of the history of the early emerging church is the main source of early Christian thought and legend.

To judge the ressurection narratives we must also understand the historiography of Saul of Tarsus. What we know of the legendary Saul comes exclusively from the New Testament—which is not a good source since it is a collection of writings that attempts to prove its own historicity within and by itself. There are no pagan sources to use as supplemental or supportive.

According to the *corpus* of documents assembled later as the Christian New Testament, Saul of Tarsus was a member of the Pharisee community—a Jewish religious group known chiefly through the writings of Josephus, the Talmud and the New Testament. They believed in a strict legalistic Judaism. As fundamentalists, the Pharisees (an Aramaic word which means "separated ones") were puritan in nature: Austerity was their hallmark and badge, fostering synagogue worship while opposing individual supplication. Their insistence on purely external observation of the Law made them unpopular with Jesus (Matt. 23.13-36), but not with people who believed they were being punished by their god for having tolerated "liberals."

After the alleged death of Jesus, many Pharisses accepted a belief in a resurrection and a retribution in the next world. Gamaliel, a Pharisee, actually publicly defended the Apostles before the Sanhedrin (Acts 5:34-40), which cost them popular support, so that when Jerusalem fell in 70 CE, they disappear from history. Today their influence survives only in the teaching of the Rabbis and the *Mishnah*.[7]

Saul's acceptance and declamations on the concept of the resurrection isn't, as Christian apologists have argued through the centuries, an "enlightenment" that took place when he "converted" to Christianity.[8] The idea of resurrection among Pharisees can be traced back to the earliest writings of pre-Maccabeean Jews.[9]

Saul is only one of the Pharisees that play a major role in the develop of the Christ legend. Two other men also appear in the New Testament: Nicodemus and "Joseph."

Nicodemus and Joseph are the two men who allegedly buried Jesus. They were also the last two men to see his body.[10]

Joseph and Nicodemus, as Pharisees,[11] were highly educated. Nicodemus was a master teacher (*rabbi*) of the resurrection doctrine.[12] The New Testament tells us that he spoke to Jesus at least once,[13] and it's highly probable that at this meeting they discussed this concept.

Joseph, we are told, was a "secret disciple"[14] of Jesus,

and saw him under the cover of darkness.[15] Joseph, like Nicodemus was devoted to the concept of the resurrection,[16] and certainly must have discussed it with Jesus who uses the Pharisean words in his discussions and as interpolated by Saul the Pharisee of Tarsus.

This brings the scholar full circle to the involvement of Saul of Tarsus in creating and embellishing the Christian legend. Evidence for this is found in both his epistles and *The Book of Acts.*

Saul hungered for peace of mind. The strict adherence to the Law wasn't fully satisfying.[17]

Leaving the rigors of Judaic life, Saul traveled to Arabia. There he spent some time observing pagan religions.

Following his sojourn to Arabia, Saul returned to the city of Damascus. It was there he changed his name to Paul. With a new name came a new dedication — pursued with the same vigor and zeal.

Believing he was "born again" (a philosophy common among Pharisees and most pagans), he went out to preach his concept of the resurrection to his one-time coreligionists, now deemed "heathens."[18]

Saul's concept of resurrection centered on and surrounded the allegedly slain Jesus. Yet Saul never saw Jesus in the flesh. He met Jesus, reputedly, only in a vision on the road to Damascus.[19] More than likely, this hallucination occured during an epileptic seizure which his contemporaries accorded divine qualities and properties to: encompassing and encircling all aspects of illusions especially the "speaking in tongues" (*glossolalia*).[20]

Saul's "observations" of Jesus were purely emotional. They weren't based on natural of physical phenomena. Therefore, Saul's "explanations" and defense (*apologia*) are allegorical or speculative at best.[21] It is upon these Pauline allegories that the early cult of Christianity created its history and *tabula.*

After the death of Saul of Tarsus the leaders of the Christian cult declared his allegories fact. On legend and fantasy a faith was built, and on the illusionary faith a concrete church crafted.

While the officials of the cult declared the death and resurrection of the alleged Jesus to be fact, non-Christians disputed it.[22] Even Saul recognized that the alleged resurrection was a "stumbling block" to the Jews, and "foolishness" to converts from paganism. It was a laughable doctrine since the pagans (*paganus*: country people) had rejected earlier tribal gods, most of which had experienced similar deaths and resurrections of their own. Paganism was never truly made illegal until 380 CE.

What troubled many pagans, Jews, and even new converts to the most recent cult to creep out of a stagnating Judaism was the fact that there was no single account of the alleged death and resurrection of Jesus. Instead, there were at least five accounts, and none of them agreed on each point. This requires us then to examine and compare the various extant commentaries (testimonials) of the gospel writers, many of whom couple concepts with more ornate Old Testament theory and prose.[23]

1.   The account in Mark 16 (ca. 70 CE)

Mark is the simplest account of the alleged resurrection of Jesus.

The account of Mark claims that *three* women went to the graveyard where Jesus was allegedly entombed. They arrived at *sunrise* on a "Sunday" morning to "anoint" the body of Jesus with "spices."[24]

What is curious is that these *three* women waited for *three* days after Jesus was allegedly buried. The temperature was high and the corpse would have been badly decomposed.

Another curiosity is that the women, apparently, knew

that the tomb was sealed with a heavy stone. They knew that they couldn't move it, yet they took neither men nor tools with them to gain entrance to the blocked sepluchre.[25]

As the women approached the tomb, they asked one another who would move the stone.[26] Perhaps they knew of a strong man — like "Legion" — who lived in the graveyard[27] and could be impressed to move it for them.

Arriving at the tomb, the three women found the stone moved.   Together, like the Three Fates, they entered the cave. Once inside, although it was dark and they had come from light, they saw "a young man" sitting.[28] What he was sitting upon in the tomb isn't clear.

The young man spoke. His words frightened them.[29] He announced that Jesus wasn't in the tomb. Further, he recounted, Jesus had left for Galilee.[30]   Galilee is 60-70 miles north of Jerusalem—a sizable distance[31] seldom travel- ed in a single day, and never on foot.

The young *man* then precisely and expressly ordered the *three* women, as a unit, to tell Jesus' disciples *and* Peter that "he [Jesus] is on his way to Galilee," and that they would see him there. There is no reference in Mark that any of the three women, less alone all of them united, told anyone anything. They didn't even mention that the body of Jesus was gone,[32] and Mark says nothing about Jesus appearing in Galilee.

Mark changes his story, and embellishes it richly. He, quite suddenly in a shift in sentence structure and thought flow, records that Jesus appears in Jerusalem, to *one* woman only.[33] She is Mary Magdalene, who, according to some, was a common woman, or even a whore. Now it's not the *three* women but the one woman, Mary Magdalene, who tells the "mourning and weeping" disciples who believed Jesus to be dead, that "Jesus is risen."[34]

Mary Magdalene wasn't good at convincing anyone. Undoubtedly hysterical, Mary Magdalene couldn't convince the disciples of Jesus that their teacher and leader was alive: that Jesus fulfilled the resurrection thesis.[35]

Contemporary Christians see no problem with this. The common argument is that the men, being torn with grief, had little interest in "good news." But that doesn't go far enough to answer why Mary Magdalene's word was ignored.

It's far more true that Mary Magdalene wasn't believed. Mark describes Mary Magdalene as having been disturbed by demons! Few people believed in the words of anyone that was "possessed."[36]

But why is Mark silent about the other three women at the tomb? And why did these three women go to the tomb to anoint the body of a dead Jesus?

Jewish law required Joseph of Arimathea, an influential counsel member of the Jewish community,[37] to anoint the cadaver before it was entombed.[38]

And if women went to the tomb, why wasn't Jesus' own mother in their number? Certainly she would have been a party to the anointing. Certainly the writer would have been precise if it had been Jesus' mother; instead he recites the trio only as "Mary, Salome, and Mary the mother of James."

Then there's the confusion about how long Jesus had been out of the tomb. There's testimony by two people that they had seen him "in another [spiritual? ghost-like?] form" walking the countryside.[39] These additional witnesses also tell the disciples what they had seen. The disciples reject their testimony and refuse to believe Jesus rose from the dead.[40] Not yet are they tied to the resurrection myth.[40]

If the disciples had believed in the truth of the accounts they would have rejoiced. They did not. They did not see the man Jesus as the son of God in mortal form. Nor did they believe he was sacrificed as a part of a greater plan to appease a jealous god/father and thus release *man*kind from Adam's alleged curse/sin.[41] Still Mark records that those who refuse to believe the "good news" of the sacrifice and resurrection "shall be damned."[42] So much for a gentle

24

Jesus! So much for a merciful and loving Father in heaven!

II. The account in Matthew 27:62-28:17 (ca. 85 CE)

"Matthew's" resurrection story is substantially different from the one "Mark" presented to us. In Matthew the tomb is supposed to be sealed the "next day" (after the crucifixion of Jesus) by Jewish authorities. A watchman is to be secured to guard it.[43] It can be argued that the Jewish elders and the chief priest thought that Jesus had foretold his resurrection,[44] and that there might be an attempt to steal the body in order for his disciples to claim that the dead Jesus had risen from the grave.[45]

In this "gospel" we also read that *two* women (unlike Mark's *three* women) went to "see" the sealed tomb,[46] and *not* to anoint the cadaver of Jesus. Surprisingly, *only* Matthew's version relates that the women experienced a "great earthquake" at the tomb.[47] In spite of the occurance of the earthquake, it *did not* shift the doorstone from the tomb and the tomb remained sealed.

Instead of natural phenomena moving the stone, it was, allegedly, "an angel of the Lord" that came down and put "his" (there are no female angels, and until the clarification of sexlessness in heaven, there are only male angels) shoulder to the stone and moved it away. At that point it is the angel (not the young *man*, as recorded in Mark) that sits down — and this time the recorder is more precise: the angel sits down on top of the stone *outside* the tomb (not inside as Mark related[48]).

"Matthew" claims that the angel's countenance is "like lightening,"[49] yet the ladies in Mark saw the young man only as "strange," and thus ignored his orders. In Matthew, they listen to the angel, and they allow the angel to show them that Jesus isn't in the tomb.[50] They are instructed to tell the disciples that Jesus is risen—and they hurry away to spread the angelic message.[51]

The *two* women in Matthew's account aren't frightened (as were the *three* women in Mark's story). Instead they went "with great joy" to tell the disciples[52] that Jesus will meet them in distant Galilee.[53]

Within moments, the writer of Matthew has Jesus appearing to *two* women on the road to Jerusalem. He repeats the message the angel had given them. In Mark, Jesus appears only to *one* woman—but then at a later time.[54] Also, in Matthew's version (which is contrary to John's account[55]) the two women immediately recognize Jesus and were allowed to touch and worship him.[56] (This is a pagan Egyptian custom associated with the rejoining of the torn flesh of Osiris by his sister-wife Isis!)

The next thing we read in the Matthew account is that the disciples are ordered to have a secret rendezvous on a mountain in Galilee—if they wish to see their risen Lord.[57] Apparently still skeptical, the disciples go to the mountain. It's there they first see the resurrected Jesus! Although the writer of this account claims that the disciples saw the resurrected Jesus—or, a human body transfigured by an indwelling spirit no longer living an earthly life—not all believed that it was Jesus, or that he rose from the dead.[58]

Recalling Jesus' orders, Matthew records that the first appearance came to *eleven* disciples on a mountain in Galilee (not in Jerusalem as it appears in Luke,[59] John,[60] and Mark[61]). That means the disciples had to cross more than 60 miles *that day* to comply with Jesus' order—in spite of the record of the words given at the Last Supper.[62]

Other points mentioned in Matthew's account contradict the other accounts. Only in Matthew can you read that the women saw a squad of soldiers trembling before the angel's "glory."[63] Later, these same trembling soldiers go to tell the high priest and his cohorts about their close encounters of the strangest kind.[64] But as eager and convinced as the soldiers are to tell their story, they are as easily intimidated to say that they all fell asleep while on duty! implying they were willing to face execution for such a treason! But this isn't the record left us.

Pilate refused to give the Jewish court a guard squad. He ordered the Jews to provide their own watchman.

The writer of Matthew ignores this, and within a few sentences transforms the Jewish watchman into a squad of guards. Another cult miracle.[66]

Not only does the writer create this slight of hand by changing the Jewish watchman into Roman guards, but he goes further. He makes them responsible to the same governor who refused, passages earlier, to have anything to do with the sordid mess.[67]

No longer is it a Jewish watchman that falls asleep on duty. It's an entire Roman squadron. And the penalty for such action is death.

At this point the writer plays into the ruse that there may have been a conspiracy between Roman guards and the Jewish council. Mutually they conspire to keep this breach of security quiet. The priests knew they could save no sentry from death if that guardian fell asleep at his post. Therefore, no mention would be made of it unless "it comes to the governor's ear."[68] A mere trifle!

The priests actions speak further. Why would Jewish authorities be worried about a "resurrection" of the man they labeled a great deceiver, while the disciples of Jesus forgot or didn't believe that the Nazarene would "rise again"?[69] This is especially critical when it comes to notice that there was rumor that many other "bodies" (zombies?) had recently risen from their graves and appeared to many in the "holy" city of Jerusalem.[70] Surely, the news of these resurrections would have helped Jesus' followers to remember their rabbi's reputed prediction that he would rise from the dead.

In face of these facts, it's understandable why the Jewish council believed a conspiracy was developing to counter and lessen the Sanhedrin's hold over the people. While their predecessors faced previous imposters and prophets, Jesus' message of cooperation with the hated enemy (he told them to put down the sword and to give to the Romans what was theirs: "render onto Caesar the things that are Caesar's....") was a direct attack on tradition and their authority.

The writer of this gospel had to make the point that the cult-followers of the "slain" shepherd would confound and confuse those who oppressed and slew their leader. At best the book of Matthew is a contrived deceit and twist of fact.

III. The account in Luke 23:53-24:54 (ca. 90 CE)

More contradictions are found in yet another "gospel." In charity we could argue that the writer of Luke wasn't privy to the same information as the other gospel authors – or wasn't an eye witness to the entire unfolding of the story of the resurrection.

While Mark records that *three* women went to the cave in which Jesus' body was allegedly laid, and Matthew details the travels and travails of *two* women who sojourned to the sepulchre, Luke claims that there were *four* women who went to anoint what should have been the badly decomposed cadaver of their folk hero.[71] Not only do the four go to the tomb, carrying spices, but in this account they also take with them "ointments."   Why these ladies would take ointments to the tomb is unknown, especially in light of the statement by the author(s) of the Luke who claim that the body of the son of a carpenter was properly prepared and interred into the tomb by no one less than Joseph of Arimathaea.[72]   Their odyssey was totally unnecessary.

When the four women in Luke's account arrive at the

place where Jesus was allegedly lain after his reputed crucifixion, they found the tomb open. The stone was moved
away. And the tomb was empty.[73]

In the Lukean account, the four women mentioned in
this gospel don't find a "shining angel" *sitting* on the doorstone outside the sepulchre, smiling at a squadron of terror-
stricken soldiers, as Matthew claims; nor do the women see
a solitary young man sitting *inside* the tomb with no soldiers
around. Instead, the writer(s) of Luke relate that *two men*
clothed in shining garments suddenly appear *standing* by the
women to tell them that Jesus "is risen."[74] Could it have
been that these *men* frightened Joanna and the other women
present *inside* the tomb?[75]

The sudden appearance of two men by the empty tomb
frightened the women to such an extent that they run home
and remind the disciples that Jesus foretold he would rise on
the third day—a detail, it appears, everyone forgot![76] But
the disciples didn't believe them—or the myth of resurrection that was more a part of the Pharisee pasttime than it was
a creed of the not yet developed cult of Jesus. The disciples,
in fact, call the tale told by the women an "idle tale."[77]
The disciples are of a like mind, in all the accounts, that the
Jesus they knew wasn't the least bit likely to rise from the
dead. And in this gospel, the women never saw an actually
arisen savior. They merely accepted it on blind faith on the
word of two total strangers who wore "shining garments"
and appeared suddenly without warning.

The writer(s) of the Lukean account go further than the
rest at this point. In this version, a skeptical Peter (who is also known as Cephas, and who was initially known as Simon
bar [son of] Jonas)[78] literally runs to the empty tomb, and
there finds Jesus' burial clothes—clothing the women didn't
discover. What Jesus was wearing when he left the tomb, according to this account, isn't mentioned. Did he walk out
naked—and remain nude throughout the rest of the gospel?

Even the Lukean account of Peter running solely to the tomb is opposed by yet another gospel, that one given the name of John. Peter doesn't run alone, according to the gospel of John: instead, Peter *runs a race* with John to the tomb and is defeated—John gets there first![79]

Later, in the Lukean account, Jesus is found walking seven miles with two of his followers,[80] presumably in his newly transfigured (unclothed?) body. That the man who is walking with the two men is Jesus is determined only by the writer(s) of Luke. The other two men didn't recognized their road companion. Jesus had to go to great lengths to prove that it was he. He had to convince them that he was ''the Christ'' who was predetermined to die and rise again—thereby fulfilling prophecy.[81]

Jesus was not, obviously, a great communicator. It took him several hours to prove to the other two men who he was. The Lukean account relates how the reputed Jesus and his traveling companions had to walk for some time over dusty roads until they came to the village of Emmaus.[82] Either convinced or very tired, the two companions of the alleged Christ rest at Emmaus, and then travel on to Jerusalem—this time quite excited. They now accept Jesus as who he claimed he was.[83]

The two men on the road to Emmaus were not a part of Jesus' remaining inner circle of eleven. They go to Jerusalem to tell the surviving disciples (Judas committed suicide) of their close encounter with Jesus.[84] But the disciples no more believe them than they did/would accept the fantastic tale uttered by the women who would return from the open cave.

Even in this there is a contradiction made more raw by variant accounts in the other gospels. In the gospels of Mark and Matthew, Jesus patently refuses to meet the disciples in Jerusalem. Instead he designates a melodramatic rendezvous in Galilee on a mountain top.[85] Luke doesn't give a meeting place. Instead the author(s) of Luke claim that Jesus appeared to the eleven inside the city of Jerusalem, where they had gathered in spite of the fact that they could all be arrested as accomplices of the crucified Nazarene.[86]

Even though the eleven had been prepared by three years of alleged miracles, they were still terrified and frightened when they ultimately saw the dead/risen Jesus.[87] The ugly marks of the crucifixion would certainly frighten anyone. Even once they got used to the gored momentos alleged to be on the hands and feet and in the side of Jesus, the disciples remained skeptical about his resurrection.[88] What finally convinced the eleven was watching him eat fish and honey—a motor function essential to any living mortal, but totally unnecessary for any god that didn't have mortal characteristics.[89] However, for gods/goddesses to eat wasn't unheard of in the days Jesus allegedly lived, for the deities on Mt. Olympus not only whored but dined, drank and partied like mere mortals, with honey being considered the nectar of the gods.

Once Jesus ate, he admonished his disciples not to leave Jerusalem until they, too, received supernatural powers.[90] This is contradicted in the gospels of Mark and Matthew.

The confusion within the sources escalates rapidly at this point. Luke says that Jesus led his distraught disciples to Bethany to witness his alleged ascension into heaven.[91] Mark has the alleged ascension taking place in Jerusalem; while in the *Book of Acts* we read that Jesus ascends from Mt. Olivet in a surrealistic "glory,"[92] while neither Matthew nor John even mention this momentous event. Their omission is fascinating, for it's the ascension that is a keystone to the total myth of Christianity.

After the ascension/nonascension, the disciples go to the Jewish temple there to worship and praise Jesus.[93] Why didn't the Jewish guards stop this blasphemy? We have no record that anything was done about this; we learn only that the disciples return to their quarters. Their they await the descent of supernatural powers, so that they too can perform miracles.

IV. The account in John 19:38-21:13 (ca. 110 CE)

The gospel called John is the newest of the officially recognized and accepted gospels of the contemporary Christian church. It was written decades after the other three official gospels.

Being a later gospel, John adds materially to the Christ legend. How much of its text is authentic is heatedly debated today, based on textual and linguistic analyses.

It's in the gospel of John that we learn that Joseph (a secret disciple of Jesus[94]) and Nicodemus anointed the body of an alleged deceased Jesus. This account renders us an account of the anointing, one which was very effective, for the text reads that Joseph and Nicodemus applied about a "hundred pound weight" (75 lbs.) of myrrh and aloe spices to the alleged corpse.[95] We also read that once the alleged Jesus' body was prepared, Joseph and Nicodemus buried it in a cave (tomb) that belonged to Joseph.[96]

The gospel of John makes it clear that Mary Magdalene *didn't* take spices to the tomb. She goes alone. It's "dark" (not dawn), and the tomb is open and the body missing.[97] The Magdalene doesn't see any angel or watchmen or even a young man (dressed or undressed). Instead, when Mary sees the tomb open and the body missing she runs home[98] and tells Peter (and John?). Hearing her message Peter and John race out to the empty sepulchre.[99] Once at the tomb neither of the men find an angel/watchmen/young man. They do see the burial clothes, and the napkin that allegedly covered the face of Jesus. ' The Magdalene was correct. The body was missing.

Peter and John don't believe that Jesus rose from the

dead.[100]   With the body gone, Peter and John feel their ties with the past master are severed. They leave. The Magdalene stands *alone*, crying.[101]   Sobbing, the Magdalene complains that someone stole the body of Jesus.[102]

Unlike the other gospels, no watchman, no young man, no angels appear the first time in the gospel of John. Instead, John says Jesus appears. It's only on her second trip that Mary sees two angels sitting inside the tomb. The angels merely ask her why she's crying. Then Jesus appears. She assumes he's a gardener, and protests that he stole the body of her lord.[103]

Angrily Jesus spits out "woman" as a verbal rejoinder. Then, Jesus softens, and whispers, "Mary." Hearing her name, the Magdalene opens her eyes and gasps, "Rabboni!" (meaning: "My Master!")—totally disregarding Jesus'earlier injunction that no *man* should be called rabbi—even the Christ.[104]

From the point of recognizing Jesus, the gospel of John begins a war of words that contradict the other gospel writers and authors.

In John, Jesus tells Mary "touch me not."[105]   In the gospel of Matthew, Mary is allowed to touch Jesus.[106]

In John, Mary returns to tell the disciples of her discovery. She, according to John, is alone in this mission.[107]

Luke says that the disciples were "terrified" when they saw Jesus. They believed he was a ghost.[108] In John, the account reads that the disciples were "glad" to see Jesus.[109]

While Matthew has Jesus appearing to the disciples on a mountain in Galilee,[110] John agrees with Luke that Jesus appears to the disciples in Jerusalem.[111]   John, alone, says that Jesus appeared twice to the disciples within the first eight days following his resurrection.[112]

Jesus appearance to his disciples is broadly magical. Like

a ghost, Jesus walks through a "shut" door.[113] Thomas, a disciple, still doubts– magicians had performed that trick for centuries.[114]

Thomas' doubts forced Jesus to take a very earthly, common approach. He had the disciple touch his wounds, and put his hand into his side.[115] (Yet the crucifixion account says that the soldier only "pierced" his flesh–not lifted it, or bore a hole big enough for a man to put his hand into the stomach of Jesus.)

Following Jesus' appearance in the "upper room" (where it's cooler at night), eye witnesses to the event testified for eight days in Jerusalem. There's no mention of prayer and praise in the temple. After this eight day ritual of testifying, Jesus returned. During this sojourn Jesus "breathed" the "Holy Ghost" on each of the men who were assembled.[116] Once hallmarked by this breath, Jesus surrendered the awesome power of absolving people's "sins."[117] But not all of the disciples used it. Seven of the disciples, weeks later, returned to the Sea of Tiberias (Galilee) there to resume their humble but honest profession of fishing.[118] These fishermen quickly forgot the "breath" and "power" given to them by Jesus. They had to be reminded again of the mission Jesus preordained for them.[119]

The fishermen became "believers" and willing servants to their master's plot, once they saw Jesus, like a common mortal, eat fish.[120] But this conversion didn't last long, either; and soon they were fishing again.[121]

In the story of the fishermen we find yet another contradiction. Matthew, Mark and Luke relate only *one* appearance by Jesus to the eleven disciples. John, details *three* appearances. And in John's record, none of these appearances makes a lasting impression, and the disciples still don't affirm their faith in a resurrection.

To firm up the faith, chapter 21 of John was written. It had to show Jesus appearing in Galilee.

V. The Testimony of Saul of Tarsus (a.k.a. St. Paul): I Corinthians 15:5-8 (ca. 56 CE)

One might think that the epistles (letters) of Saul of Tarsus—some of which were composed at least thirty years *before* the oldest gospel—would provide us with the most reliable information on the alleged post-resurrection appearances of Jesus. But they don't. As Saul, himself tells us, he never met Jesus in the flesh. He only had a vision—which occured, most likely, during an epileptic seizure.[122]

Epilepsy was considered a "sacred" state, during which time anointed priests and representatives of deities communed with the god(s) of the land. It's during one of these seizures, or possibly hallucinations common with weary travelers, that Saul determines the "proof" of Jesus' existence, message, and resurrection.

Like many Pharisees, Saul has an engorged ego. It's for this reason that this man from Tarsus tells us that he was the *last* witness to a post-crucifixion appearance of the mortal from Nazareth.[123]   It's on this statement that Christian apologists argue that Saul's testimony is both complete and historically accurate. But is it?

Saul's testimony is tainted by his own existence. He went by many aliases. He was a common murderer, consenting to the slaying of Stephen known as the First Martyr (or witness), and the execution of many others.[124] A genocidic maniac, Saul served as a member of the High Priest's band of armed thugs.[125] Even when Saul "accepted" the divinity of Jesus, this mortal was quick to lash out in anger violently destroying or maiming his enemies. Thus, when the Jewish magician bar Jesus posed as a prophet and openly opposed Saul's teachings of the new messiah, bar Jesus was struck blind at the instance of the raving Apostle.[126]

A one-time tent maker,[127] Saul seldom forgot his baser roots. Although born in what is today modern Turkey,

Saul was "born" a Roman citizen: a title he carried with some pride and gratification—for it put him subject to Roman courts and Roman jurisprudence, and outside of the more venal courts of the priestly class in Jerusalem.[128]

Like other apologists for the Christian cult, Saul fails to give dates or precise locations for various testimonies. For instance, Saul says that Jesus was seen first by *Cephas* (Peter or Simon bar Jonas) immediately after the resurrection—*not* by Mary Magdalene, as most of the other accounts give.

Once Saul states that Cephas saw Jesus, he writes that Jesus then appears to the other *twelve* disciples. There are two problems here. One: Judas had already died. Two: there were never more than twelve disciples, and with the death of Judas, only the other *ten* could possibly have seen Jesus.[129]

Saul continues by claiming that Jesus then exposed himself to another 500—all at the same time. This account and number doesn't appear in any of the traditional/accepted gospels.

After Jesus appears to the 500, according to Saul, Jesus then appears to James, and then again to all of the disciples, and finally to Saul himself, some years later, during one of Saul's numerous visions/hallucinations.[130] This was apparently a sign to an unbelieving Jew—in direct contradiction to Jesus' vow that no sign would be given to Saul's generation or nation.[131]

Saul doesn't say why James was singled out to have an individual and private viewing of the resurrected Christ. Nor does Saul mention Mary Magdalene as being an eye-witness, while the authors of Matthew, Mark and John do. Further, Saul fails to mention Jesus' encounter with the two men (Simon and Cleopas) on the way to Emmaus.[132] And Saul never mentions the empty tomb!

As for the resurrection, there's not a single eye-witness account given by Saul. Still Saul salutes the resurrection and claims that it's proof that believers also will rise from their graves on "judgment day."[133]

Supposedly, Saul died around 64 CE, spending his last few years in prisons and under house arrest.[134] He was charged with the crimes of inciting rebellion, civil disobedience, and profaning the Jewish temple.[135] During this time it's likely that Saul experienced deep feelings of guilt, confusion, and uncertainty because of the religious intolerance he exhibited towards his neighbors and co-citizens throughout most of his life. He wrote: "I do not do the good I want, but the evil I do not want is what I do. Wretched man that I am!"[136]

Epilogue

Saul was like his coconspirators. Disillusioned with their own reality, they attempted to create one from fantasy.

It's in the writing of Saul of Tarsus, and those penned by the scribes of the authors of the gospels, that the world has built a cult as brittle as century-old sunbaked clay tablets. The accounts of the resurrection are without consistency, and yet they're offered as infallible proof that Jesus died and was raised from the dead.[137]

At best the story of the resurrection of Jesus is a myth. Like other pagan beliefs, Christianity was invented by intimidated men, and practiced by those who wanted a firm answer to the troubling questions of life.[138]

Christianity would never have survived the rise of Mithraism and other eastern oracle-fed religions if it hadn't been for the "vision" experienced by the Roman emperor Constantine who didn't want to offend *any* god. Jesus was never historically singled out for primacy or absolute rule over the hearts and minds of mortals by the emperor. Constantine who died a pagan/atheist as he was born was quite aware of the plethora of expanding, suffocating mystery religions plaguing his empire. Constantine was also aware that each of these new eastern cults had the same themes in common. That all of their gods were born, died, and rose again from the grave. Even the early Christians didn't deny this truth. They only claimed that it was the illusionary, mythical Devil that inspired pre-Christian nations to accept the resurrection myth.

The name Jesus, itself, is tied to lore, legend, and the grappling of a troubled people pleading for some assurance and stability. Jesus is a variant of Joshua (*Jeschu*). Joshua/Jeschu was the ancient Hebrew sun-god who was demoted to human status by the priests of a petty, angry god known as YHWH (Yahweh or Jehovah). It was on this sun-god that Christianity developed, personifying the golden orbe of the sun into a son of man.

The mysterious doctrine of the Trinity is easily explained, and done away with. The Trinity is no more than a transmogrification of the sun-god syndrome: Since there can be no life without sunlight, the sun became known as the legendary Creator/Father. And, without adequate sunlight things die, so the sun became known, as well, as the protector or preserver of life (unless there is too much sun which then destroys life), both of which give rise to the concept of good and evil, sin and grace. And it's by sunlight mortals see, read, and learn, and thus the sun is also the Teacher/Ghost. And the trinity—or three faces (*persona* or characteristics) become divine, and the Trinity is considered three-in-one, united.

Huntington, West Virginia
25 December 1989
The Vernal Equinox

NOTES

[1]While no material in this essay is totally the original analysis of the author as no work of scholarship and research is at any time, it's presented to help others understand the contradictions in the most famous legend in the Christian world: the resurrection of Jesus. I acknowledge my endebtedness to the written words of Joseph McCabe, and to numerous telephone conversations with Dr. Arthur Frederick Ide.

[2]Aramaic is a Semitic language that was common at the time Jesus allegedly lived, having been the basic language in Northern Syria and in Mesopotamia. It was used throughout the Levant for commercial and diplomatic transactions (see: 2 Kings 18:26). Hebrew, as a language, was cultivated only by a few of the most learned. Today, Syriac is a form of this language, as is Mandaic.

[3]Flavius Josephus' Ιουδαικη Αρχαιολογια is composed of 20 books which trace the history of the Jews from "creation" to the end of the Jewish war. The early books repeat the legends of the Old Testament. Later he incorporates the writings of Dionysius of Halicarnassus and Nicolaus of Damascus, as well as Apocryphal works. His most famous reference to Jesus is in XVIII:3.3, where he calls him "a wise man, if indeed one should call him a man," but this line is in doubt, being questioned as to its authentic authorship by serious scholars. The best critical edition of his works is edited by B. Niese (6 vols. and index) published in Berlin (1887-1889). Loeb issued a translation by H. St. J. Thackeray in 1926.

[4]See Niese.

[5]Eusebius, *Hist. Eccl.* I:ix.7f.

[6]See: Arthur Frederick Ide, *The Problem of An Historical Jesus* (Toronto: Theological Inquiry Press, 1979).

[7]Julius Wellhausen, *Die Pharisaeer und die Sadducaeer* (Berlin, 1874). Emil Schuerer, *Geschichte des juedischen Volkes im Zeitalter Jesu Christi* (4th ed, 1907) II. pp. 449-475.

[8]This assumption is based on I. Cor. 15:12-17, and John 6:54.

[9]Cp. Acts 23:6-8 with Dan. 12:2. An early, medieval treatment, was given by Thomas Aquinas, *Summa Theologica* III, qq.54: "De Qualitate Christi Resurgentis," and 56: "De Resurrectionis Christi Causalitate." While Christian apologists argue that the concept of a resurrection is unique with the ministry of Jesus the Jewish bible, the Old Testament, gives numerous examples of the same theory (see. Isaiah 26:19, Job 14:13-15, and 19:25-26); cf. Acts 24:15.

[10] John 19:38-39.

[11] John 3:1: Ην δε ανθρωπος εκ των Φαριζαιων Νικοξημος ονομα αυτω αρχων των Ιουδαιων.

[12] John 3:9-10.

[13] John 3:2.

[14] John 19:38.

[15] John 3:2; since he was a "secret disciple," it is logical that he spoke with Jesus only at night or in secret meetings.

[16] Mark 15:43 and Luke 23:51.

[17] Phil. 3:9.

[18] Gal. 1:16-18.

[19] Acts 26:12-19.

[20] Cf. Acts 2:4. Later Saul was suspicious of those who "speak in tongues" since they couldn't translate nor disclose the meaning of what they said; he later decried this phenomenon, contrasting it sharply with prophecy (see: 1 Cor. 14:1f) and urged Christians to foresake the *glossolalia*.

[21] Gal. 4:21-24.

[22] 1 Cor. 1:18-23.

[23] Deut. 18:22 recognized the problem early.

[24] Mark 16:1-2. In this sentence the word is αρωμα (aromatic/sweet spice)

[25] Mark 16:3.

[26] Mark 16:3.

[27] Mark 5:1-9.

[28] Mark 16:5. In this sentence: νεανισκος, meaning "in the prime of life;" probably a teenager.

[29] Mark 16:5.

[30]Mark 16:7.

[31]Mark 11:39.

[32]Mark 16:7-8.

[33]Mark 16:9: Αναστας δε πρωι πρωτη σαββατου εφανη πρωτν Μαρια τη Μαγδεληνη παρ ης εκβεβληκει επτα δαιμονη.

[34]Mark 16:10.

[35]Mark 16:11: κακεινθι ακουσαντες οτι ζη και εθεαθη υπ αυτης ηπιστησαν.

[36]Mark 16:9, 11.

[37]Mark 15:43,

[38]Mark 15:46-47 and John 19:39-40.

[39]Mark 16:12: Μετα δε ταυτα δυσιν εξ αυτων περιπατουσιν εφανερωθη εν ετερα μορφη ποπευομενοις εις αγρον here we see the word μορφη (morphe).

[40]A classic on resurrection theology is: Robert Henry Charles, *A Critical History if the Doctrine of a Future Life in Israel, in Judaism and in Christianity* (Jowett Lectures for 1898-1899; New York: AMS, 1979. reprint of 1899 ed.).

[41]Mark 16:11, 13 and John 14:28. Saul of Tarsus elaborated on the "sin' of the biblical "Adam": Rom. 5:12-15 and 1 Cor. 5:21-22.

[42]Mark 16:16: ο πιστετσας και βαπτισθεις σωθησεται· ο δε απιστησας κατακριθησεται· σημεια δε τοις πιστευσασι ταυτα παρακολουθησει· Note: κατακριθησεται is the κατακρινω ("to judge one down"). Compare this with Saul of Tarsus curse in Romans 14:23.

[43]Matt. 27:62-66.

[44]Matt. 27:63.

[45]Matt. 27:64.

[46]Matt. 28:1.

[47]Matt. 28:2: και ιδου σεισμος (seismos) εγενετο μεγας.

[48]Mark 16:5.

[49]Matt. 28:2 *vs*. Mark 16:5.

[50]Matt. 28:3, 6.

[51]Matt. 28:6.

[52]Matt. 28:8.

[53]Matt. 28:7,

[54]Matt. 28:9-10: cp. Mark 16:9.

[55]John 20:17.

[56]Matt. 28:9.

[57]Matt. 28:10, 16,

[58]Matt. 28:17.

[59]Luke 24:36.

[60]John 20:19.

[61]Mark 16:14.

[62]Matt. 26:32.

[63]Matt. 28:4.

[64]Matt. 28:11.

[65]Cp. Matt. 27:65 with Matt. 28:12-15.

[66]*Ibid.*

[67]Matt. 27:19-24.

[68]Matt. 28:14.

[69]Matt. 27:63.

[70]Matt. 27:52-53.

[71]Luke 24:1, 10.

[72] Luke 23:53, 56.

[73] Luke 24:2-3.

[74] Luke 24:4, 6.

[75] Luke 24:5.

[76] Luke 24:8.

[77] Luke 24:11: και εφανησαν ενωπιον αυτων ωσει ληρος τα ρηματα ταυτα και ηπιστουν αυταις here we find ληρος which can also be translated as "idle tales" or "folklore." The idea of "resurrection" was known by many to be a mystery ritual/rite: a fantasy for initiating neophytes into select circles.

[78] Luke 24:12. According to John 1:35-42, Simon bar Jonas is introduced to Jesus by his brother Andrew, and given the name "Cephas," which is more than likely the Aramaic equivalent of the Greek πετρα or "rock" (Peter). His name appears first in all lists of the Twelve, and is always present on all occasions when only a "small inner group" was called (Matt. 9:18-26, 17:1-8, and 26, 37). He is given certain supernatural abilities, such as walking on water (Matt. 14:22-33, and speaks for the others as their mouthpiece on several occasions (John 6: 66-69; Luke 22:31). For further information on Peter and how his own cult followers propelled the concept of the "Petrine Doctrine" of primacy, supremacy and infallibility to the bishop of Rome, see: Arthur Frederick Ide, *An Apology for the Petrine Doctrine* (Cedar Falls, IA: University of Northern Iowa, 1968) and C. Heussi, *War Petrus wirklich roemischer Maertyrer?* (1937). Eusebius wrote on him in his *Hist. Eccl*, II:xxv, 5-8; and Irenaeus, *Adv. Haer.* III.i, 2 and III:iii, 1,who gives him a special authority.

[79] John 20:4.

[80] Luke 24:13-34.

[81] Luke 24:25-27.

[82] Luke 24:18.

[83] Luke 24:32.

[84] Luke 24:33-34.

[85] Cp. Matt. 28:16-17 and Mark 16:7 with Luke 24:36.

[86] Luke 24:37.

[87] Luke 24:37.

[88] Luke 24:41.

[89] Luke 24:42-43: Εχετε τι βρωσιμον ενθαδε οι δε επεδωκαν αυτω ιχθυος οπτου μερος και λαβων ενωπιον αυτων εφαγεν.

[90] Luke 24:49.

[91] Luke 24:50-51.

[92] Acts 1:9-12.

[93] Luke 24:52-53.

[94] John 19:38.

[95] John 19:39-40.

[96] Matt. 27:60.

[97] John 20:1.

[98] John 20:2.

[99] John 20:4.

[100] John 20:7, 9.

[101] John 20:11.

[102] John 20:11, 12. When Mary looks into the tomb, she sees *two* angels, snd even then complains that the body was stolen (John 20:13).

[103] John 20:15; cp. Matt. 28:8-9.

[104] John 20:16: the prohibition against calling anyone rabbi is found in Matt. 23:8.

[105] John 20:17.

[106] Matt. 28:9.

[107] John 20:20.

[108] Luke 24:37.

[109]John 20:20 cp. Luke 24:37 which argues that the disciples were terrified at seeing Jesus after the alleged resurrection.

[110]Matt. 28:10.

[111]John 20:19. Only the apostle Thomas doesn't go to the mountain.

[112]John 20:26. Two appearance during the eight day ceremony of the Black Mass was traditional at this time.

[113]John 20:26.

[114]*Papyri graecae magicae*, 2d ed., edd. K. Preisendanz and A. Heinrichs (Stuttgart, 1973-1974) 1,178f; going through locked doors in XII,160ff, 279; XII,327ff. 1064ff; XXXVI,311ff. See also: Philostratus, *Vita Apollonius.*

[115]John 20:28-29.

[116]John 20:22.

[117]John 20:23. Peter (Simon bar Jonas) was given this power much earlier; see: Matt. 16:18-19.

[118]John 21:3.

[119]John 21:4f.

[120]John 21:9-13.

[121]John 21:11.

[122]2 Cor. 12:1-8. See also: Arthur Frederick Ide, *Saul of Tarsus* (Toronto: Theolog·ical Inquiry Press, 1978), pp. 69-72.

[123]1 Cor. 9:1.

[124]Acts 7:58-60 and 8:1-3.

[125]Acts 9:13-14 and 26:11-12.

[126]Acts 13:4-12.

[127]Acts 18:3.

[128]Acts 21:39 and 22.27-28. See glossary for discussion. (p. 100)

[129]1 Cor. 15:5-8 cp. Acts Matt. 27:5 based on Acts 1:18. There is a problem concerning the "discipleship" of Jesus. Allegedly twelve men, it is also claimed in Luke that Jesus had 72 followers that he sent to various cities (10:1).

[130]Acts 26:13-19. Saul frequently hallucinated ("had visions") which no one else was privy to, yet the foundation of Pauline Christianity if founded on these hallucinations.

[131]Mark 8:12.

[132]Luke 24:13, 28, 34.

[133]Phil 3:11. Judgment Day, as a theological concept, can be dated back to early Egyptian civilizations, as well as to antecedents in eastern civilizations centuries before. See: Smith, *The Secret Gospel*, 17. Cp. M. Eliade, *Shamanism* (New York: Pantheon Books, 1964). In this case, as throughout the legend of Jesus, people, like their pagan counterparts, "go up to the mountain" to meet and/or be judged by "god." See: *Apollonius* III.13 *vs* Ezek. 28:12ff and Isaiah 14:13ff, 1 Enoch 14:8ff and 71, 2 Enoch 3-10.

[134]Acts 24:27; 27:1 and 28:16, 30.

[135]Acts 24:5-6.

[136]Rom. 7:19-24.

[137]David Friedrich Strauss, a German theologian, first applied the "myth theory" to the life of Jesus in his classic *Leben Jesu*. It denied the historical foundation of all supernatural elements in the gospels. His last work, *Der alte und der neue Glaube* (1872) negates Christianity in favor of scientific materialism amd rejects human immortality. Strauss is joined by French philosopher and theologian Joseph Ernest Renan, author of *La Vie de Jesus* (1863), which also repudiates the supernatural elements in the life of Jesus, and portrays him as an amiable Galilean preacher. This skepticism was carried on by Rudolf Bultmann, a German New Testament scholar and theologian, who authored an elaborate analysis of the gospel sources in his *Die Geschichte der synoptischen Tradition* (1921; enlarged 1931). Among the more conservative-traditionalist writings is *The Doctrine of the Incarnation* (1848) by Robert Isaac Wilberforce, who joined the Roman Catholic church in 1854, and at the time of his death (1857) was preparing for the priesthood.

[138]Richard Adelbert Lipsius, *Ueber den Ursprung und den aeltesten Gebrauch des Christennamens* (Jena, 1873). Arthur Frederick Ide gives two important studies in the development of the early church in his *Martyrdom of Women*, as cited, and his *God's Girls: Ordination of Women in the early Christian and Gnostic Churches* (Garland, TX: Tangelwuld, 1986). See also his: *Teachings*

46

of Jesus On Women (Dallas, TX: Texas Independent Press, 1984), and his *Jews, Jesus & Women* (Mesquite, TX; IHP, 1984).

The desire for established, immovable, infallible answers has not only buttressed the Roman Catholic church, but is the backbone of today's Protestant evangelical churches. Thus G. Marion Robertson ("Pat" Robertson) issued his *Answers to 200 of Life's Most Probing Questions* (Toronto: Bantam Books, 1984), with other televangelists following suit. As Dr. Ide points out in his biography of the preacher-turned-politician-turned-show host-turned-politician, many of these "answers" are not only biblically unjustifiable but a sham.

There is no tangible, historical proof that Jesus rose from the dead. It is as speculatory as Robertson's pat answers.

Many gods besides Jesus have allegedly died, been resurrected, and ascended into heaven. This idea is as old as time and as current with contemporary non-Christian faiths as it was with primitive tribes. It all goes back to the harvest and replanting and regeneration of crops and of other plant life.

Serious scholars have found that centuries before the alleged time of Jesus, the eastern Mediterranean nations annually celebrated the death and resurrection of numerous gods, including Osiris. Tammuz, Dionysus, Quetzalcoatl, Baal-Taraz, Adonis, Attis, Apollonius, and Mithra. The early Christians never denied this; they only claimed that the "devil" inspired the "pre-Christian" nations with the resurrection myth.

The name Jesus, as has been shown is a variant of Joshua (*Jeschu*), who is the ancient Hebrew sun-god. This god was demoted to human status by the priests of Jehovah (YHWH), and on it Saul of Tarsus founded his Christian cult. So, let me say—as did Saul of Tarsus—that if Jesus wasn't raised from the dead, then nobody will be, and "your faith is also vain." (1 Cor. 15:12-17).

ON THE NON-EXISTENCE OF GOD

by Joseph S. Zemel

For thousands of years, the majority of the human race has believed in some sort of diety.[1] Theists have claimed that the deity in which they believe exists. They argue that it's not just a mythological character, or one created by warped, unrealistic imaginations.

Ancient gods, now called mythological characters by most "civilized" people, were as real to the ancient Greeks, Romans, Egyptians and other premodern people, as are the modern gods, such as Allah, Jesus, Buddha and the like, believed to be real to twentieth century mortals. While most contemporary religions don't spend a great deal of effort, time and resources attempting to prove the existence of their deities, Christians seldom exercise this good sense. Instead they spend generations of various resources in an attempt to prove the existence of that which they can't see, hear, touch, feel, or demonstrate scientifically. Christians, historically, place faith above and over reason. The truth of the matter is that the techniques of logic can disprove the Judeo-Christian god(s) as simply as it disproves the totem tokens of the cob-webbed past.

Logic, as a term and as a discipline, is defined today as "the science concerned with the principles of valid reasoning and correct inference, either deductive or inductive."[2] To be "logical," the individual must know *and* understand the laws of logic.

The first law of logic is the *Law of Identity*. This law states that "anything is itself." For example: If item "A" is an apple, then item "A" is an apple.

The second law of logic is the *Law of Excluded Middle.*

50

This law states that a statement is either true or false. There is no middle ground. For example: "A piece of paper *is* a piece of paper." It is true, in and of itself. It's not sort of true: "A piece of paper is a slice of blueberry pie."

The third law of logic is the *Law of Contradiction.* This law states that something can't be true and false at the same time. Using the last example: The piece of paper can't be both a piece of paper and a slice of blueberry pie at the same time.[3]

A valid system of belief must be based on indisputable knowledge. In order for knowledge to be "true knowledge" (as opposed to "false knowledge" — or propaganda shrouded as truth), it must be tested according to the properties ascribed to true knowledge. For a belief to be classified as true knowledge:

(a) A belief must be based on evidence.

(b) A belief must be internally consistent (that is: not self-contradictory.

(c) A belief can't contradict previously validated knowledge with which it's to be integrated.[4]

"God" is defined as: "One of various beings, usu[ally] male, in mythology, primitive religions, etc., conceived of as immortal, embodying a particular quality or having special powers over some phase of life."[5] This definition is best suited for the general term "god."

Understanding the Judeo-Christian god requires familiarity with the attributes of that god. The Jewish god is defined as "Was, is, and will be. He caused everything to be. Without him nothing can exist. There is no end to his attributes. He is all the attributes."[6] The Christian god is defined as "almighty, eternal, holy, immortal, immense, immutable, incomprehensible, ineffable, infinite, invisible, just, loving, merciful, most high, most wise, omnipotent, omniscient, omnipresent, patient, perfect, provident, supreme, true."[7]

Many people believe in a god because of "faith" or "belief without need of certain proof."[8] "Faith" is the justification used by many theists to rationalize to themselves and to others a belief in a nonapparent deity.

"Faith," by definition, is a belief that *has not been proven.* To accept the belief in a god by faith is to accept the belief in a god without proof.

If we use faith instead of logic to acquire knowlege, we will never be sure of anything. If logic enables us to find the truth, then there is no need for faith.

> *Reason does not permit an alternative method of acquiring knowledge. The principles of reason are intended to separate justified from unjustified positions: if a belief cannot meet the requirements of reason, it is unjustified—without sufficient foundation —and must be condemned as irrational (e.g., contrary to the requirements of reason). Faith, by its very nature as belief in the absense of rational demonstration, must also be condemned as irrational. In this context, "nonrational belief" is irrational.*[9]

By ascribing attributes to an entity, that entity becomes limited and confined by those attributes. If one of an entity's attributes is that it needs oxygen to live, then that entity is limited by that need. The same is true for the attributes of a deity. All those attributes serve to limit the deity.

There are two different attributes: *Positive* attributes

(those that describe what an entity is), and *negative* attributes (those that describe what an entity is not). The negative attributes of the Judeo-Christian god were created to prevent that god from having limitations. The problem with this premise is that by stating that a being has a certain quality, it's prevented from simultaneously having the opposite quality. For example: If an entity is invisible, it can't be visible concurrently. Another major problem with negative theology is that through it a god is being given the same attributes as nonexistence. If you use only negative theology to describe any being, there is no way to distinguish that being from nothingness. "God is not matter; neither is nonexistence. God is not visible; neither is nonexistence. God does not have limitations; neither does nonexistence. God does not change; neither does nonexistence. God cannot be described; neither can nonexistence."[10] According to negative attributes, God is identical to nonexistence.

The positive attributes also limit "god." They come from human experience. God is not human, therefore god cannot have human experiences.

When an attribute that is finite is attributed to an infinite being, it has no meaning. For example: When a theist says that god is a living god, does that mean that god is living the same way that we know of life? Anything that is living must also die. Does this mean that god must die? God is said to have unlimited knowledge. Living creatures get knowledge from experience, errors of others and errors of their own. Does this mean that god errs? If so, then god must be limited —as is man. If attributes don't mean the same thing when applied to natural entities as to god, then "they assume some unknown, mysterious meaning and are virtually emptied of their significance."[11]

God is supposed to be ineffable (or, "indescribable").[12] God is also supposed to be incomprehensible. If god is supposed to be ineffable and incomprehensible, then god has no attributes. The only way something can be known is by its being able to be described. Theists give god unlimited attributes, but if god has unlimited attributes then god is describable and comprehensible as well as indescribable and incomprehensible. Not being able to comprehend and describe god prevents god from being examined using logic or rational techniques, thereby making the concept of god irrational.

God is also supposed to be almighty or omnipotent. This attribute was given to god to make god have unlimited powers. However, being omnipotent is logically impossible. If god were omnipotent, god would be able to do anything. If god could do anything, then god can tie a knot that he can not untie. God would be able to be totally invisible while being totally visible, everything while being nothing, and true while being false. All of these examples are self-contradictory. By being self-contradictory, they violate the rules of logic and knowledge and are, therefore, illogical and irrational. The arguement is, therefore, absurd.

In addition to all these attributes/nonattributes, the Judeo-Christian god is thought to be omniscient (or "knowing all things").[13] If god is all knowing, knowing all things, then god knows the entire past, the present, and the future. This is a direct contradiction to god's attribute of omnipotence. If god knows the future then neither god nor man can change the future. If god can't change the future, then god is not all powerful. If god can change the future, then god does not know the future. God can't be both omnipotent and omniscient, because both qualities together are self-contradictory. God also, if omnipotent, would automatically be omniscient. This is also a contradiction. If god can't be both omniscient and omnipotent, then god must be neither. If god is neither omniscient nor omnipotent, then god is not god and therefore does not exist.

God is supposed to be omnipresent (or, "the quality of

being everywhere present at the same time").[14]   If god is omnipresent, then god is limited.   The statement that god is everywhere disproves god's omnipotence.   If god is everywhere, then god does not have the ability to be in only one place at one time.   If god is omnipotent, god therefore must be omnipresent, because if god is able to do anything then god is able to be everywhere at all times.   If god is not able to be both omnipotent and omnipresent, then god must be neither omnipresent nor omnipotent.   Therefore, god not having the attributes of god, can't be god.

God is supposed to be omnibenevolent (or, "all good").[15]   The Judeo-Christian god is shown throughout the Old and New Testaments to be everything and anything but good.   He has killed the first born male of the Egyptians.[16]   He turned a woman into a pillar of salt because she dared to turn around to look at her home being destroyed by this same loving god.[17]   He dropped 250 men, women and children into a pit for not believing that Moses was his representative on earth.[18]   And, there are hundreds of other examples in the Jewish and Christian bibles, and supplementary tracts and commentaries.

Allegedly, the god of the Christians and the Jews speaks to his "faithful" out of "his" bible.   While this god is acclaimed to be a loving and forgiving "father" there are few passages that show him to be either loving or forgiving.   On the contrary, the god of the Judeo-Christian bible(s) is evil, cruel and sinister.   The Judeo-Christian bible records laws which, if no observed to the letter, warrant a death penalty.   All that can be said from these injuctions, laws, and penalties is that the Judeo-Christian god is the ultimate expression of masochism and cruelty, for there is a plethora of means and ways to dispatch the unfaithful—depending upon what crime/sin was committed.

The sins or crimes damned by Judeo-Christian god(s) are many.   They include witchcraft,[19] violating the sab-

55

bath,[20] committing adultery,[21] blaspheming,[22] cursing one's parents,[23] and numerous others.[24]

The Judeo-Christian god(s) is/are blood-thirsty. He/ they told the ancient Jews to kill all of the members of the tribe of Amalek—men, women, and children—without warning.

How can this god be considered "good"? Yet both Jews and Christians call their god "good." This is lunacy!

But taking the Judeo-Christian concept that their god(s) is/are good, it should stand that he/they can do only good or ask people to do good. If his/their laws are good, then this/ these good god(s) must slay all those who violate the sabbath today—or about 99% of the mortal race. He/they would also have to execute all children who don't do what their parents demand—regardless of the age of the child or the mental condition of the parent, including parents who are senile or suffering from Alzheimers Disease! That would be at least 50% of the population. And this/these same good and merciful god(s) would have to wreck vengeance and take the lives of those who commit adultery—at least 10% (to 55%, depending on which statistic you're looking at) in the United States alone. So. too, must this/these gentle savior(s) kill those who blaspheme, or fail to keep the "jot and tittle" of the myriad of his/their other laws and contradictions scattered like dung thrown to the wind through his/their holy book(s). Of course, if mortals followed the bible as it demanded, and if the god(s) also didn't miss a cue, most of mortalkind would not be here today!

In addition to the paucity of examples of a loving, forgiving and merciful father in the Judeo-Christian bible, we find nature filled with numerous examples of a god that doesn't always create good—assuming, from the Judeo-Christian perspective—that such a fiction actually exists. There are with us at various times hurricanes, earthquakes, diseases, and uncounted other things that hurt, harm or kill those "created in his image." If god is responsible for what happens, or if god is powerful enough to prevent it—and does not—then god is not all good. A succinct summary of the problem of an "all good" (omnibenevolent) god is given to us by George H. Smith:[25]

> If God does not know there is evil, he is not omniscient. If God knows there is evil but cannot prevent it, he is not omnipotent. If God knows there is evil and can prevent it but does not desire to, he is not omnibenevolent. If, as the Christians claim, God is all-knowing and all-powerful, we must conclude that God is not all-good. The existence of evil in the universe excludes this possibility.

The Jews and the Christians bring 10 arguments to attempt to prove the existence of God. The arguments are:

(1)   First Cause (or, "Cosmological Argument")

(2)   Design (or, "Teleological Argument")

(3)   Argument from Life

(4)   Argument from Revealed Theology ("Bible")

(5)   Argument from Miracles

(6)   Argument from Religious Experience

(7)   Ontological Argument

(8)   Moral Argument

(9)   Wish Argument

(10) Argument from Faith.

The *First Cause* argument states that: "Everything must have a cause. Therefore, the universe ["the whole creation embracing all celestial bodies and all of space"[26]] had a cause, and that cause was God. God was the first (or, "uncaused") cause."[27] There is a major problem with this argument. If the universe needed a cause, and that cause was god, then who made god? If everything is created by something, then god must have had a creator, who in turn would have required a creator, infinitively. If god doesn't require a creator then the universe doesn't require a creator, either. If the universe doesn't require a creator, then it is not self-evident that a god created the universe.

Another problem with the *First Cause* argument is that there are certain things that happen to everything in the universe that doesn't happen to the universe as a whole. For example: Everything in the universe is over and under an object. The universe itself isn't over or under any object, because, by definition, all objects are contained within it. If there are certain things that reflect items in the universe but not the universe as a whole, then creation could be one of them.[28]

The argument from *Design* states that "the universe is wonderful and exhibits evidence of design or order. Things which show such wonderful design must have had a designer even more wonderful. That designer is god." This argument has a major fallacy. If god is the greatest thing, then something even more wonderful than god must have made god. If nothing made god, then the premise that everything has a designer is false.[29]

The *Argument from Life* states that "life cannot originate from the random movement of atoms, yet life exists. Therefore the existence of a god was necessary to create life."[30] This argument has the same problem as the *Argument from Design* and the *First Cause* argument. If god is

58

alive, and something must have created life, then something must have created god. What about deformed people? Did god make a mistake? Life was not created by chance, but created by a combination of the "non-random laws of chemical physics."[31]

The *Argument from Revealed Theology* states that "the Bible states that God exists, and the Bible is the inspired word of God. Therefore, what it says must be true, and God does exist." If we are trying to prove that a god exists, we can't use the bible as proof. That is begging the question. Calling the bible the "word of God" is also not allowed because we have not proved that god exists. This is a circular argument.[32]

The *Argument from Miracles* states that "the existence of miracles ["an event that appears to be neither a part nor result of any known natural law or agency and is therefore often attributed to a supernatural source"[33]] requires the presence of a supernatural force (*i.e.*, a God). Miracles do occur; therefore, there is a supernatural force or God."[34] Just because someone can't explain something according to present knowledge doesn't mean that with further investigation he or she wouldn't be able to do it. Five thousand years ago people couldn't explain the rainbow. It was considered a miracle. Now that we have the knowledge of light infraction to explain a rainbow, we know it's no miracle.

The *Argument from Religious Experience* states that "many people have claimed to have had a personal experience or encounter with God; therefore, He must exist."[35] The feeling of this experience is called "mysticism." It's the "doctrine or belief that through contemplation and love man can achieve a direct and immediate consciousness of God or of divine truth, etc., without the use of reason or of any of the ordinary senses."[36] Those who use this argument are confusing a feeling of having met god with the fact of having met god. Mysticism isn't a rationally valid procedure for attaining facts. It eliminates reason.

The *Ontological Argument* states that "God is, by definition, perfect. A necessary quality of a perfect object is that it exists (if it does not exist, it would not be perfect). If perfection requires existence then God exists."[37] The previous statement is begging the question. It states that if something has a definition then it exists. This need not be true. A definition can be created for anything; that does not make it true.

The *Moral Argument* states that "all men have moral values. The existence of these values cannot be explained unless they were implanted in man by a God. Therefore, God exists."[38] If this were so, then all people would have the same moral values. Morals are taken from the society. People two thousand years ago had different morals than we have. Most people consider slavery immoral today; two thousand years ago it was common and considered good—and in some cases "holy," as "god" told the "chosen people" to make slaves of those they conquered.[39] Therefore, if morals are from god, then either it is moral to have slaves (as in the bible) or not to (as in the present day).

The *Wish Argument* states that "without the existence of a God, man would have no reason to live or to be good. Therefore, there has to be a God. Most people believe in a God, therefore there is a God."[40] A thousand years ago most people thought the world was flat. Now we know it is "round." Just because they thought it was true one thousand years ago, does not make it true. Also, people don't need god to make a reason to live. Many people don't believe in any god and have a reason to live. Some people live for their children or their spouse. Others live to accomplish something (being a good doctor, or lawyer, for example). People don't need a god to have a reason to live.

The *Argument from Faith* states that "the existence of God can not be proven by the use of reason, but only by the use of faith. The use of faith shows that there is a God, therefore, God exists."[41] As we have proven, logically, before, faith is not a valid way to obtain knowledge. Faith does not *prove* that any god exists.

There is no logical way for the Judeo-Christian deity to exist. I deny the existence of Zeus, Minerva, Apollo, Hera, Vulcan, Thor, and all the ancient gods. Most intelligent people deny the existence of these gods. Jesus and the Judeo-Christian gods are just more gods, and I deny them as well. The only difference is: I deny one (or two or three) more gods than they. My denial of the Judeo-Christian deity (or deities if you wish to consider the "Trinity" as three-gods-in-one) is based on logic. He (or their) alleged existence is not based on evidence. It is self-contradictory. It contradicts previously validated knowledge that it's attempting to be integrated with. Therefore: God does *not* exist.

Philadelphia, Pennsylvania
10 December 1989

NOTES

[1] James G. Frazer, *The Golden Bough: A Study in Comparative Religion* (London: Macmillan, 1890) 2 vols. Reissued as *The Golden Bough: the Roots of Religion and Folklore* (New York: Anvel Books 1981; distributed by Crown Publishers). This is a classic study in superstition.

[2] Funk & Wagnalls Publishing Company, Inc. *Funk & Wagnalls Standard Encyclopedic Dictionary* (Chicago: J. G. Ferguson Publishing Co., 1975). p. 381.

[3] George H. Smith, *Atheism—The Case Against God* (Buffalo, NY: Prometheus Books, 1979), p. 143.

[4] George H. Smith, *Atheism—The Case Against God*, p. 103.

[5] *Funk & Wagnalls Standard Encyclopedic Dictionary*, p. 275.

[6] Personal interview with Rabbi Pesach Oratz, 25 November 1987.

[7] Felician A. Foy, O.F.M., *1987 Catholic Almanc* (Huntington, IN: Our Sunday Visitor Publishing Division, Our Sunday Visitor, Inc., 1988), p. 298.

[8] *Funk & Wagnalls Standard Encyclopedic Dictionary*, p. 228.

[9] George H. Smith, *Atheism—The Case Against God*, pp. 110-111.

[10] George H. Smith, *Atheism—The Case Against God*, p. 52. See also: Jon Murray and Madalyn O'Hair, *All the Questions You Ever Wanted to Ask American Atheists* (2d ed.; Austin, TX: American Atheist Press, 1986), pp. 30-31, 36-39, 42, 46-47, 58-59, 73, 86-87. 99-100, 134ff.

[11] George H. Smith, *Atheism—The Case Against God*, pp. 55-56.

[12] *Funk & Wagnalls Standard Encyclopedic Dictionary*, p. 331.

[13] *Funk & Wagnalls Standard Encyclopedic Dictionary*, p. 455.

[14] *Funk & Wagnalls Standard Encyclopedic Dictionary*, p. 455.

[15] *Funk & Wagnalls Standard Encyclopedic Dictionary*, p. 59. Cp. Thomas Aquinas, *Compedium Theologiae*, Pt. 1, cap. 141.

[16] Exodus 12:29.

[17] Genesis 19:26.

62

[18]Numbers 16:31.

[19]Exodus 22:18.

[20]Exodus 31:14-15.

[21]Leviticus 20:10. See also: Arthur Frederick Ide, *The Holiness Code and the Devolution of Woman* (Toronto: Theological Inquiry Press, 1977).

[22]Leviticus 24:16.

[23]Leviticus 20:9. See also: Arthur Frederick Ide, *Vows, Virgins, Oaths & Orgies* (Arlington, TX: Liberal Arts Press, 1988), pp. 23-37.

[24]Murder: Jeremiah 7:9, Hosea 6:9; idolatry: 2 Kings 23:5, 2 Chronicles 15:16, and others. The infamous "Holiness Code" is found in Leviticus, which includes "god" "setting his face against" those who eat blood (17:10), engage in adultery (20:10), practice magic (20:6), undress the aunt of one's own mother (20:19), and so on.

[25]George H. Smith, *Atheism—The Case Against God*, p. 81.

[26]*Funk & Wagnalls Standard Encyclopedic Dictionary*, p. 745.

[27]Gordon Stein, ed., *An Anthology of Atheism and Rationalism* (Buffalo, NY: Prometheus Books, 1980), p. 56.

[28]B. C. Johnson, *The Atheist Debater's Handbook* (Buffalo, NY: Prometheus Books, 1983), p. 62.

[29]Gordon Stein, *An Anthology of Atheism and Rationalism*, pp. 56-57.

[30]Gordon Stein, *An Anthology of Atheism and Rationalism*, p. 57.

[31]Gordon Stein, *An Anthology of Atheism and Rationalism*, p. 57.

[32]Gordon H. Smith, *Atheism—The Case Against God*, p. 57.

[33]*Funk & Wagnalls Standard Encyclopedic Dictionary*, p. 414.

[34]Gordon Stein, *An Anthology of Atheism and Rationalism*, p. 57.

[35]Gordon Stein, *An Anthology of Atheism and Rationalism*, p. 57. The original argument was originally posed by Thomas Aquinas, *Summa Theologiae*, pt. 1, quaes. 2, art. 1, c.

[36] *Funk & Wagnalls Standard Encyclopedic Dictionary*, p. 431.

[37] Gordon Stein, *An Anthology of Atheism and Rationalism*, p. 58.

[38] Gordon Stein, *An Anthology of Atheism and Rationalism*, p. 58. This argument was brought into vogue by the early mediaeval monk Anselm of Canterbury.

[39] 2 Kings 2:14, Isaiah 49:11, 45:13, 20:4. Ezekial 1:1 are some examples of slavery but where various words denoting "captive" was used. The word "slave" appears in Tobias 10:10; Judith 3:4, 4:10, 5:11, 6:7 and 10, 7:27, 8:7 and 22, 9:3 and 10, 10:23, 12:10, 13:1, 14:13 and 18; Wisdom 9:5, 18:11, 19:14 and elsewhere. Slavery was a definite part of the society, as witnessed in Judith 8:23, Additions to Esther 14:8, and 2 Maccabees 5:14 and 8:10. It was scriptural interpretation in antebellum America that led many ministers, especially Baptists, to justify and fight for slavery in the United States, causing a split between the northern and southern religious bodies. See: Arthur Frederick Ide, *Evangelical Terrorism* (Irving, TX: Scholars Books, 1986), pp. 28-29, 37-38. It's interesting to note that the *Encyclopedia of Southern Baptists* (Nashville, TN: Broadman Press, 1958) totally ignores the role slavery played in Baptist history.

[40] Gordon Stein, *An Anthology of Atheism and Rationalism*, p. 58.

[41] Gordon Stein, *An Anthology of Atheism and Rationalism*, p. 58. This argument stems from Thomas Aquinas, *Summa Theologiae*, I, 2, 3, c, who went on to argue that without faith there is nothing, including charity or reality: in his, *Summa Theologiae I-II, 65, 5*, c: "Et sic caritas sine fide et spe nullo modo esse potest." This is both the negation of observation and the surrender of reality to surrealism and fantasy.

THE PHYSICAL JESUS

by Arthur Frederick Ide

Hollywood Director Martin Scorsese's movie, *The Last Temptation of Christ*, created a furor in the Christian community even before the film was released. Christians reacted to this celloid fantasy in the same manner as Moslems reacted to the publication of Salman Rushdie's *Satanic Verses*.

Censorship became the goal of both religious cults. Censorship is, by its very nature, a prop to hold up a decaying and mind-destroying system, On the other hand, censorship does add some life, however staid, ossified, and putrifying, to a theory, government or other institution that can't maintain its own existence. While the unholy Inquisition pulsed through Europe's Middle Ages, the Roman Catholic church survived and grew. When more than a few dared question and popular rage rose up against the corrupt and barbaric practices of the Inquisition, the church teetered. With its weakening, Martin Luther and other reformers broke away from this suffocating motherload.

While Luther and his co-religionists in the Protestant camp attempted to set up a new "evangelical" order, not all of the faithful were willing to follow them blindly into another mental prison. Some, like Thomas of Muenster, demanded that each man be his own priest, and to divest the world of the scourge of a ecclesiastical heirarchy and the trappings of an organized church. Still, like all religious hypocrits, Muenster was not opposed to establishing his own order.[1] For his troubles, Muenster, like other reformers, would be labeled "the Great Satan," "Satan," and the "Devil." Their assumed threat to order was more than those trembling in power could stand.[2]

Muenster's detractors would have felt quite comfortable

in the mind-melt of radical religionists who worked feverishly to stop the distribution and showing of Nikos Kazantzakis' classic work. It was Kazantzakis' intent to give Jesus a more human form.[3] To fulfill the very creed of Christianity that Jesus was "true man." But this idea, fulfilled, was more than the cultists could understand, appreciate, or accept.

The cult followers were terrified of the thought that their idol, Jesus, could have been or be characteristically mortal. They refused to entertain Scorsese's reasoning behind the filming of Kazantzakis' important work. As the beseiged director told *Time* magazine reporters, the screening of *The Last Temptation of Christ* was his way of "trying to get closer to God."[4]

Christian cultists, like other fanatics, would not tolerate dissent, or even accept the fleshing out of their own ideology and theology. Instead, seeing and perceiving their petty deity as a brutal, vengeful and weak godhead, one who would damn others but could not defend himself, they raced in to take charge and protect their imposter. As many of the radical right roared, they would take "Christ over the Constitution!" for democracy meant nothing to them, nor did First Amendment rights. Thus, John Evans, representing the religious right in the pseudosophisticated city of Dallas, Texas, noted, he "and my family won't be seeing this movie." He would make the decision for those he felt he was "in charge of" as if he were their own lord and

John Evans, Dallas Mayor pro tem

master. The tragedy of the Evans eclipse of reason is that he was but one dark cloud covering the torch of liberty and the light of reason. Dallas, a collection of small enclaves of reactionism and radical hatred of anything that would suggest democracy, is led into the pig pen of preacher pushed censorship, an enslavement of the human mind, by its self-serving city council. A council of corrupt politicians, it voted 10 - 0 to "urge" Universal studios to recall the film. Not surprising, none of the council members had seen the film. But the Dallas City Council traditionally votes in the blind, buffeted by total ignorance. It's subservient to the blue-nose purists who run roughshod over the Constitution which the Dallas District Attorney's office considers a needless and dangerous document. When not listening to the DAs, the Dallas City Council gives credence to the words of self-styled, self-appointed, and usually self-ordained "evangelists," such as Ira Green. Green's legendary as a bitter pulpit pounder who never saw the movie, but felt qualified to condemn it as a "satanic attack" against Jesus and his followers. He was joined by another weasel waltzing to the funeral music of organized religion: the "reverend" R. Wayne Brashear, senior minister of the Urban Park Assembly of God church in Dallas. Brashear claimed that the movie depicted Jesus as an emotionally demented, mentally unstable, hypocritical, bisexual adulterer: "This movie defames our Lord and Savior," he concluded in an ejaculation of eccentricism.

Like Green, Brashear never saw the movie—nor planned to do so. He was joined by televangelist Mike Evans—more at home in theater paint than a parish pulpit. As "pastor" of the Church on the Move in Euless, Evans promised to picket the film, defying the First Amendment. He was joined by such radical reactionaries as Tom Hinton, youth minister at Bethesda Community Church in Fort Worth, and Russ Houck, executive director of Christians in Action—a group founded to erase First Amendment rights in the United States.

In Mesquite, Texas—legendary for its neofascist government and venal cops—the City Council hurriedly met on
Monday afternoon, 19 September 1988. The purpose was
simple: to ban all showing of *The Last Temptation of Christ.*
The censorship of Scorsese's masterpiece was but one more
nail that the Mesquite City Council drove eagerly into civil
liberties as they pilloried the First Amendment.

Michael Lenz, legal counsel for the Dallas office of the
American Civil Liberties Union noted the situation clearly.
The Mesquite City Council resolution showed "abundant
ignorance of the Bill of Rights."[5] It further illustrated how
far the corrupt Mesquite government would go in suppress-
ing liberty.

The Mesquite City Council resolution openly defying
First Amendment rights, not only exiled the movie from any
theater wishing to show it in the one-horse, rodeo-oriented
town, but directly defied and condemned the historic princ-
iple which once made the United States great. It tore down
one more brick in the wall separating state and church.[6] The
Mesquite ordance reads, in part: "...the City of Mesquite is a
family-oriented community that believes in the Judeo-Christian moral values that formed our nation in its beginning
[sic].... ... in the City of Mesquite, there are 85 church con-
gregations with thousands of members who contribute in a
positive way to the moral climate of our city ... there is grave
concern *among the religious community* throughout our
nation over the motion picture, 'The Last Temptation of
Christ,' because the movie portrays Jesus Christ as a struggling
fool and fornicator, which is an attack on their deeply held
religious views...."[7]

Controlled by hot-headed demagogues, the Mesquite
City Council pandered to the mentally enfeebled while
libeling the discerning who they refused to allow to judge
the movie for themselves. The resolution states that the
City Council "encourages the *decent* citizens of Mesquite to
refuse to attend those local movie establishments which

ignore the legitimate concerns of the religious community and show this picture."[8]   By this, the Mesquite City Council made several key points:

(1)   Only Jews and Christians have morals.

(2)   Judeo-Christian "morality" is to be forced on everyone.

(3)   85 churches control the city.

(4)   The only "decent" people in Mesquite are those who refuse to view *The Last Temptation of Christ.*

(5)   The "concerns" of religious people (that is: those who attend church) have greater value and weight than the concerns of those who don't attend church or subscribe to the fascist dictates of the Mesquite City Council.

Lenz judged it correctly: "This is nothing but pandering to the religious right. The problem is that the moderates [and liberals] have abandoned the political field.[9]   When Mayor George Venner was called on it, he refused comment. Other city councilmembers went so far as to argue that anyone who supported the showing of the film was "in league with the Devil," while anyone who had seen the movie "had sold his [or her] soul to Satan." The Mesquite police vowed that if they found the movie in anyone's home, they'd arrest the owner of the house for possession of pornography and seek their indictment.   Several cops even vowed to "plant" the movie (or other "pornography") in private homes in order to "get rid of the godless liberals" who were demanding basic liberties.

Fort Worth, Texas, had even more unusual problems. One-time Tarrant County Republic Party Chairman Jim Ryan told reporters that he was stepping down from his job rather than com-promise with "satanic" GOP party members who would not come out publicly and conemn the controver-sial movie about the physical life of Jesus. He resigned during a Tuesday night party meeting after a move he led to condemn *The Last Tempta-tion of Christ* was voted down by 1 vote.

Jim Ryan

Suffering defeat, Ryan had only negative words for his copolit-ical companions: "Either you are on God's side, or Satan's side. They [those who voted against his resolution to condemn the movie] are against *anything* that's Christian." Going further, Ryan called those who opposed him "satanic people."

Intolerant of all dissent, he criticized the media for not taking a more definitive stand against the movie. When he found little support, and increasing opposition at home, he slipped back into his usual name-calling, labeling those who'd disagree further with his totalitarian views "communists."[10] The battle was joined.[11] The "reverend" Andy Radke of Ennis, Texas, initiated a boycott against MCA Universal of-fices in Dallas,[12] while thousands of screaming religious fanatics protested at Universal Studios in California.[13] Quickly the virus spread, drowning out the sound of those who urged reason and stood on the side of the First Amend-ment.[14]

In Salt Lake City, the movie was stolen the day before it was to be shown. The screen on which it was to play was slashed.[15] The fires of censorship caught on everywhere as fundamentalists fan the flames of ignorance while lighting torches to ignite bales of books, films and papers that carry a message they refuse to hear. And their Christ is dead, both in history and in their hearts, as they transmogrify the message "Seek you the truth, and the truth shall make you free." Instead these bibliolators bend the knee and bow the head to the cold and lifeless god of unreason, captured in the cell of censorship, and spew back like vomit their own message of hate coupled with the writhing words of "see not," "read not," "go not," and "think not." They're supported by pretend-jurists who have a Christian timetable and sit enthroned in ignorance on cold state and federal benches in Tennesse, Alabama and Dallas, determined like Hitler to weed out dissent.

Evangelical fanatics feign to forget that their own original godhead was "true *man*." Yet it is the manhood of their alleged savior that made this reputed being noteworthy nearly two thousand years ago—albeit to a mere handful of people. But this handful found enough excitement in the manhood/godhood of their alleged savior to "go out to all nations, preaching and teaching" the message millions today believe he elucidated.

But if their Jesus lived, and if in fact he was true man, does it not demand that this mortal being be as other mere mortals? Would not this Jesus, this true man, urinate, defecate, masturbate, and sweat?

If the alleged Jesus lived, would he not know the grip of passion, the lingering longing for love and companionship? Would not this alleged Jesus give vent to anger, sorrow, want, disappointment, affection—in fact the true and pulsating, probing plethora of human feelings that sets the evolutionary species *homo sapiens* apart from other creatures whose psychology we have not yet learned or even begun to study?

And if the Jesus of the fundamental evangelicals was

in fact and not just in legend "true man" and did truly die, why do they ignore his begging to be spared death, his anger while supposedly nailed to the cross, and his passion to place his mother and his beloved John in one another's care? It is because today's Christians, like those throughout history, want an antiseptic god—a clean god—a fairytale god who doesn't have erections, doesn't seek sex, doesn't know hunger or thirst, but is somehow, illusionarily immortal while being mortal.

The Jerry Falwells, Pat Robertsons, and Wallie Criswells have placed a legend on a pedestal, worshipping the image they created to match their own insecurities and uncertainties. They demand that others yoke themselves to their base absurdities, for the Jesus these evangelical preachers preach into the stagnating minds of their flock of gospel geese could never have lived, breathed, or died. Their savior wasn't crucified by Roman soldiers, but by the stupidity and baiting of the mesmerized masses who willingly allow others to turn reality upside down. Although these predatory preachers verbally ejaculate the dead semen of fiction, they've been countered by one mortal who had more belief in his disbelief or uncertainty than they have enjoined collectively in their televangelistic crusades to conquer and destroy reason. As Nikos Kazantzakis wrote in his preface to *The Last Temptation of Christ*: "The dual substance of Christ— the yearning, so human, so superhuman, of man to attain God, or, more exactly, to return to God and identify himself with him—has always been a deep inscrutable mystery to me. This nostalgia for God, at once so mysterious and so real, has opened in me large wounds and also large flowing springs." And then admits the reason he wrote and published his ultimate classic: "This book is not a biography, it is the confession of every man who struggles. In publishing it I have fulfilled my duty, the duty of a person who struggled much, was much embittered in his life, and had many hopes. I am certain that every free man who reads this book, so filled as it is with love, will more than ever before, better than ever before, love Christ."[16]

Scorcese's film followed the legend of Jesus. More than anyone else, save Kazantzakis, Scorcese has given the world a testament of love. This is because love is not sheltered, nor hidden, forbidden or ignored, covert or something to be ashamed of. Instead it is open, and open to all things, and it is sexual. It is in sex that mortal beings reach their highest moment of giving of themselves while sharing with another if the act is done in and coupled to love, emotion, empathy, sympathy, pathos and eros.[17] For this reason, if Jesus ever did exist, and people wish to claim that "Jesus is love," than, it too must be recognized that Jesus was sexual if he was human.[18]

To being human and within the realm and reality of love, there is a multitude of means and expressions of that love which all are a part of and intricate with sex and sexuality. The range is from a mere touch, to a kiss, to a sharing of one's self, and the ultimate expression: orgasm. Each one is a unit, and together they create a perfect unit that any mortal can understand and relate to. Chief among these is the kiss.

The Kiss

The disciple Judas has been condemned by theologians and lay Christians for "betraying" Jesus with a kiss. Yet within the Christian bible, this "betrayal" was foretold—in fact, commissioned by "god." How then can it be evil—unless god is evil? Yet, it is claimed, god is good. Therefore the kiss, and Judas, must also be good.[19]

In the Greek New Testament, Judas kisses Jesus. This, the kiss, is φιλεω (phileo). The word means "to be friendly."

$\Phi\iota\lambda\epsilon\omega$ does *not* mean "betrayal." It doesn't even connotate any form of "turning in a enemy of the state"—such as the now increasing phenomena of "Judas betrayals" of parents and children by parents and children in the current hysteria of William Bennett's "drug war." The common concept of a "Judas kiss" is more appropriate when discussing the slaughter of students following the abortive Tianneman Square revolution, or the numerous instances in contemporary America. The Christian bible is clear, that the kiss of Judas was a friendly and loving gesture—such as performed by Mary who washed the hands and feet of Jesus[20] and the kiss given to the wayward son who abandoned the farm for the pleasures and promises of profit in Jerusalem.[21] Jesus even calls him "Friend" after Judas gave this kiss.

This famous kiss isn't detailed. Matthew merely states that "he kissed him."[22] Mark is equally ambiguous.[23] Luke records that Judas only "drew near to Jesus to kiss him," but doesn't state that Judas kissed him.[24] John says nothing about the kiss. John only comments that Judas "betrayed" him—a betrayal that caused Simon bar Jonas (Peter) to pull out his sword and slice off the ear of "the servant of the high priest."[25] John is the most unreliable source—having been written at least one generation after the fact.

All that the bible tells us of the kiss, is that it was "thorough". $\kappa\alpha\tau\alpha\phi\iota\lambda\epsilon\omega$. Bassed on this, and early Christian iconography, we must assume that it is the antecedent for the mediaeval *osculum pacis*: a kiss upon the mouth. The original use of $\kappa\alpha\tau\alpha\phi\iota\lambda\epsilon\omega$ was "to be very thorough" or "extremely friendly."[26] This could mean a prolonged kiss, or a "deep kiss." It overtly implies some eroticism. There is no biblical account, or other written record, that Jesus was either repelled by such a probing kiss, nor that Jesus rejected such familiarity from one of the twelve men he kept company with.

On the contrary, the bible states specifically that Jesus reprimanded those who did not kiss him. He found greater satisfaction in the display of the kiss than he did in acts of charity, as when "the woman that was in the city, a sinner, when she knew that he sat at meat in the Pharisee's house, brought an alabaster box of ointment, and standing behind at his feet, she began to wash his feet, with tears, and wiped them with the hairs of her head, and *kissed* his feet, and anointed them with the ointment."[27] When his male followers didn't follow suit, Jesus repuked them sharply: 'You gave me no kiss, but she, since she came in, has not stopped kissing my feet.'[28]

Jesus accptance of the kiss wasn't lost on Saul of Tarsus (Paul). In fact, Saul rejoices that he was kissed by many men: "And there was much weeping among them all; and, falling upon the neck of Paul, they all kissed ($\kappa\alpha\tau\alpha\phi\iota\lambda\epsilon\omega$)[29]

Theologians who argue that the kiss was "strictly platonic", or "brotherly" as reconciled in the Old Testament (*nashaq*[30]) is self-deceptive and illusionary. Nor was the now famous "Judas kiss" as a mark or recognition[31] meant to be a one-time phenomena. Jesus told his disciples, according to New Testament accounts, that those who believed in him had to "give up" everything they had and follow—"do as"— him.[32] The kiss sealed the commitment. "Brotherly," non-erotic or passive kissing marking a friendship was known as *philema*.[33]

The only objection that Jesus had to the kiss, was its paucious nature. There wasn't enough of it.[34] The anger he exhibited in this reference is the same rebuke Jesus hurled at his disciples that had joined him for dinner at the Pharisee's home.[35] It was Jesus objection to imperfect kissing that stayed with the early Christian community, who translated it as "passing on the Holy Ghost" which escaped from one believer's throat into another's when the kiss was exchanged between believers.[36]

The sexual nature of the Nazarene

The bible is clear on the manhood/earthly existence of Jesus and how he was tempted and coped with temptation. The most biting account, around which Kazantzakis wove his tale and Scorsese created his masterpiece, was Jesus' exile for forty days during which time the Nazarene was "tempted."

During the forty days Jesus fasted. He ate nothing. He must have been hungry until even the pains of hunger were consumed from within. Today we know that both historically and medically, hunger—especially acute hunger—can generate and heighten the intensity of hallucinations. Research shows us that fantasies fashioned because of hunger are usually sexual in nature.[37] The authors of the gospels, especially that known as Luke, state that Jesus experienced numerous temptations while fasting.[38] It would be poor analysis to discard the great probability that some of these delusions were sexual.[39]

Even when Jesus talked with the Devil, it is more than likely that Jesus felt the agony of unfulfilled sexual needs, for according to scripture the Satan was fond of taking on various anthropomorphic forms. Many of these deceits were in the fashion of a woman.[40]

Jesus, unlike the majority of his countrymen, was not a sexist. Women weren't taboo, eventhough his contemporaries isolated themselves from women.[41] The book of Luke notes that Jesus didn't reject women—and that he personally attended them, at times. We read: "all the women that had any sick women with diverse diseases brought the [women] to Jesus. He laid hands on every one of them... and devils went out *from many....*"[42]

Jesus wasn't afraid to touch women, either, in spite of the prohibitions in the Holiness Code. This gives birth to numerous questions, the primary one being: What was Jesus' sexual preference. The answer springs from careful analysis and interpretation of what little record still exists today.

Evidence for Jesus being bisexual does exist. There is no evidence that he was asexual. Asexuality is unnature. Sex occurs in nature. Men, like women, are sexual beings. If Jesus was "true man," then Jesus would also be sexual.

What we do gather from the crumbs in the New Testament about the sex life of Jesus is that he lived, nearly exclusively, with men. And he had three favorites within his initial discipleship of twelve.[43] The three men Jesus favored were James, Peter, and his "beloved'' John.

Women were seldom admitted into Jesus' inner circle. In part it may have been because society was exclusionary. The two genders of the mortal race remained a part until passion rose and generations of future prayers, fighters and workers were needed. Another reason may have been because Jesus was quite intimate with the men with whom he kept company. The beloved John was known to lay his head upon the chest of the Nazarene.[44] John did this frequently—especially when Jesus and the men ate together.

The exact character of John isn't easily determined. But there is one other man who has a similar rapport with Jesus. Lazarus. Today we have enough information to speculate that Lazarus and John were one and the same.

Lazarus was a young boy—or a youthful male.[45] The first we really know of Lazarus is when Lazarus dies. His death doesn't trouble Jesus. He waited four days before he "raised" the youth from his tomb.

Jesus indifferent attitude towards the dead Lazarus troubled many of Jesus' disciples. Few could understand why Jesus waited so long, noting that Jesus ''loved'' the youth.[46]

Using external works, it's not difficult to understand the lethargy of Jesus. It is extremely probable that Jesus was just carrying out a part of a pagan ritual worship service common in the Roman world. It has all the markings of being a part of the famous "Black Mass.''

In the Roman world the Black Mass was a particular and peculiar ceremony that served as an initiation rite for young males wanting to enter select societies of older men. Youths who wanted to matriculate into older circles where there were preferences and stipends given, had to attend clandestine meetings in upper rooms, in dungeons and blackened chambers. It was during the final phase of the Black Mass that the youths were ceremoniously dispatched—by way of mock murders and crucifixions, after suffering various tortures: being whipped, crowned with thorns, having their clothes torn off their bodies and their seamless garments divided between the spectators who served as sentries to guard the doors from would-be intruders who would not understand the ritual. At the end of the initiation, the future members were given vinegar to drink from sponges, and paraded among the jeering crowd.

Once the youths were "sacrificed," (during which time the initiates would cry out to their fraternal fathers, "Why have you betrayed me,") drugs would ease them into a coma-like sleep. At that point the High Priest of the secret order called upon the initiates' patrons (or sponsors) to carry the dead "warrior" (in Hebrew: "messiah" (in Greek it is the $M\epsilon\sigma\sigma\iota\alpha\varsigma$[47]) a word that also carried the definition of "leader") to a dark tomb to sleep until the potion wore off. The most handsome member was then robed in white and told to sit with the comatose until the youths awakened.

The Essene community, of which Jesus may have been a part from ages 12 to 30 (the "missing" years), had a similar ritual. The Essene initiation rites included an anointing with herbs and spices, a washing with special funeral cloths, and a final emersion known as baptism.[48]

In both cases it took three days—considered a special and sacred number- for the initiate to "rise" from the dead. This would account for the slowness of Jesus' movement to Bethany and the ultimate "resurrection" of Lazarus.

When Jesus finally arrives at Bethany, he's still not in a hurry. He goes to the home of Mary and Martha. Allegedly, Lazarus was the brother of Mary and Mother. What isn't clear is the nature of the brotherhood. Was it biological or fraternal?

Only after Jesus visits with the two women—which may have been a courtesy call, or another step in the ritual awakening—Jesus moves slowly towards the family crypt. Nearing the tomb, Jesus is assaulted with cries of anguish from those who had assembled. They couldn't understand his lack of haste, especially as many noted, "Behold how he loved him."[49]

Once Lazarus is "returned" to the living, we read no more about him. His nomenclature, or title, of being "the beloved" now switches to John. This too was a common practice of the mystery rites associated with the Black Mass, as it is with the elevation and installation of a pope. The neophyte, now received as a full member (or 'congregant') discards the "old life" by adopting a new name.[50]

From the raising of Lazarus on, we read about "John the Beloved." Was Jesus gay?

Homosexuality has been a part of every society. It is more common in cloistered communities, especially within societies separated by gender.

But homosexuality may only be a part of this story. The gospels tell us that when Jesus was "crucified" (a possible reenactment of a Osirisian mystery ceremony to further strengthen the faith of new members), he gave his beloved John to his mother Mary. There are two answers to this troubling passage. One: Jesus may have been following custom. It was common for fathers to leave the custody and care of their children to their parents if at least one of the parents was still alive. If this was the case, Jesus would have had to have married and propagated. The most likely "wife" would have been either the Magdalene or Martha.[51]

Martha would be the most ideal candidate for Jesus' wife. She cooked for him, while Mary, possibly his daughter and the sister of Lazarus, stayed and sat at the feet of her father—a custom common in all societies.

The Magdalene may have been his wife, since she did bathe his feet—another custom generally practiced at love feasts by near kin who "humbled" themselves before a lord or husband, whereas during general gatherings the practice would be done by a servant or a lesser guest who wished to advance in the group.

The actual commissioning of "adoption" was not heard by any of the recorders personally. Instead, they all watched "from afar off" while the translation of love took place and John/Lazarus was given to mother Mary.

Parent and family man.

If Lazarus/John was the son of Jesus (celibacy wasn't highly regarded even among the priestly class), Jesus would have had to have some family experiences. This is in keeping with the Jewish emphasis on the family and the injunction that all men "go forth, be fruitful, multiply."

While there are too few references to home life in the gospels, a few do exist. The most commonly known instance is Jesus sojourn to Bethany and his reception in the house of Mary and Martha.

When guests arrived, the women prepared food. While Martha went to the kitchen, Mary stayed back to listen to the words of this recently recognized and locally celebrated rabbi. [52] If Martha had been Mary's mother, Mary would have broken one of the ten commandments—obedience to a parent. The intimacy of the account shows some family tie. This could mean that Martha was Jesus' wife, and Mary and Lazarus their children. This would explain why he could admonish Martha and salute Mary's choice to stay and listen. Visitors had no right to correct hosts or their children.

The record that Jesus approached the "family" tomb is equally noteworthy. Strangers and passing prophets seldom visited places of death. Entering tombs was an action reserved for family and close friends.

When Lazarus dies, Martha sends for Jesus. She didn't believe he was god, for if she did, she would have only needed to ask him to return Lazarus to life.

When Jesus arrives in Bethany, Martha is distraught. It is she, not Mary, who rushes out to see Jesus, announcing that her once ill "brother" now was dead. Mary stays in the house as any obedient child would.[53] This would be in accordance with Jewish custom that required women to "sit in shivah." But this is the account given in the *official* gospels. In the *Secret Gospel of Mark* Mary does emerge and is promptly and angrily rebuked by the disciples while Jesus listens silently. When this account was suppressed by the fast-growing cult, it also erased it from the original *accepted* account of Mark—leaving it to appear only in the Fourth Gospel (John), and then truncated to meet current needs by a stratifying society and emerging clergy.

Nudity and the Nazarene

Another aspect of human sexuality is nudity. As a family man, Jesus would have seen his son Lazarus/John nude if at no other time, during the infant's circumcision.

Nudity was common in the age of Jesus, so much so that generations earlier the canonists had to outlaw the practice of women reaching out to grab the penis of a man.[54] Jesus himself was not a stranger to it: from his baptism by John the Baptist, to his encounter with the nude man in the garden.

Mark presents a most interesting picture of Jesus and nudity. While Jesus was waiting for Judas in the garden, a young man (Lazarus/John?) stepped out of the bushes and exposed himself to Jesus. The critical passage reads. "a certain young man followed, having a linen cloth cast about his [recently] naked body, and they [Temple soldiers] laid hold of him. But he, casting off the linen cloth, fled from them naked."[55]

The young man most certainly must have been Lazarus/ John. The record states that Jesus took a gathering of his disciples with him. Since he had allowed Lazarus/John to rest his head on his chest during the Last Supper, it is most likely that he would have taken this "beloved disciple" with him to his living wake. Why Lazarus/John took off his own clothes is left to speculation. But sexuality can't be discounted. Sex has always been a part of intimacy, affection, and closeness. It frequently takes place on the eve of a departure.

The linen cloth is also noteworthy. It was a special linen: *sindon* ($\sigma\omega\delta\omega\nu$: a muslin). It is the same garment that was wrapped around Jesus before he was laid in the tomb.[56]

Sindon is a costly linen. It was worn only by the affluent—or given as a token of love from one lover to another. It was not a traditional linen used in burials.

Burial linen was *othonion* ($o\theta o\nu\iota o\nu$). This particular linen was easily enriched with spices to stay the odor of decay,[57] and wasn't a linen used in religious rites,[58] or in uniforms of government.[59]

Othonion was a costly linen. It was also fragile.

Othonion could be used to bandage the wounded. It was sometimes used to mop up the blood of the dying or dead. It's use, however, was forbidden criminals who were either stoned or crucified.[60] Thus, Jesus could not have been buried in *othonion* linen.

The study of the linen's role in the crucifixion leaves numerous questions unanswered. But from the few details we have in the *recognized*[61] accounts, we can get a more clear picture of the human side of a near-legendary Jesus.

The "Beloved"

There are only two people that the gospels recognize as being "the beloved" of Jesus. Both are men.

Lazarus, by name, appears only in the gospel of John. In John, Lazarus appears closer to Jesus than any of Jesus other disciples.

Lazarus, in the Johnian account, is seen as a threat. When the High Priest decides to kill Jesus, Lazarus is also to be murdered.[62] Their attempts to terminate Lazarus is because they saw Lazarus as being overly active for and with Jesus.

That Jesus loved Lazarus is plain in the account. Jesus, alone, didn't believe that Lazarus had died. He knew he was only asleep—as a part of a love ritual. Jesus blithely dismissed the thought of those near him who argued that Lazarus was dead. He said, according to the gospel of John, "This sickness isn't death, but for the glory of God."[63] It is $\delta o \xi a$ (which means a form of recognition for fame, as in $\delta o \xi a \zeta o \mu a \iota$) which Jesus had condemned the "hypocrits" for (cf. Matt. 6.2). To prove this, Jesus prolonged his stay at the Jordan, so that Lazarus would be apparently "totally" dead. The death of Lazarus was to serve a purpose—one which builds on the resurrection myth that encompassed the secret societies prevalent at that time. Jesus said: "Our friend Lazarus sleeps; but I['ll now] go, that I may awaken him out of that sleep."[64] This is a standard phrase in mystery school initiations: Jesus, the older man, would awaken his lover. He was demonstrating a symbolic death and rebirth: Lazarus was to be "born again."

The tomb in which Lazarus lay was a surrogate womb from which he would come when the second birth was completed. Jesus participation in this incident is identical to the role and activities of other magicians who used symbolic rebirth (or baptism) to initiate and strengthen their neophytes.[65]

The fact that Lazarus is singled out for this experience points to the privileged position he had with Jesus. No other mortal had this preferential treatment—even the rich man who begged Jesus to spare his daughter's life was told to go home on faith. Jesus didn't raise her from the "dead." How can it be any different than the fact that Lazarus is "he whom Jesus loved"?

Since this story appears only in John, and was expunged from the other gospels, can there be little question that John was also Lazarus? The protomedieval mystic Carpocratians (2nd century CE) knew this and made it a center of their piety—until they were savagely put down by the organized orthodox church. It must be noted that the love shared between the two men is repeatedly told in the story left by John. Even the citizens of Bethany publicly proclaimed their love affair.[66]

Interestingly, the author of the gospel of John at no point in the record calls himself "John." Instead, the author refers to himself only as "the beloved disciple" and "the one whom Jesus loved."

After Lazarus' "resurrection" the name Lazarus disappears from the record. He had been "born again." Yet this man "whom Jesus loved" appears from then on without a name but only the nomenclature "the believed disciple," as witnessed in the passionate proximity of "the disciple whom Jesus loved" at the Last Supper: "Now there was leaning on Jesus' bosom one of his disciples, whom Jesus loved." It was for this reason that "Simon Peter therefore beckoned to him, that he should ask who it should be of whom he [Jesus] spake." The "beloved disciple" "then lying on Jesus' breast saith unto him, "'Lord, who is it?' "[67]

The fact that "John" was also "Lazarus" has been known for a long time by scholars.[68] It's been denied by televangelists and those who fear the revelation that Jesus was gay.[69]

Contemporary Christianity, as it was throughout its past history, remains insanely fearful of the revelation that Jesus was gay. This is because such a revelation would take from the Christian arsenal its mightiest weapon against gays and lesbians: the Christian denial of heaven to homosexuals. Yet the contemporary Christian need turn only to his or her bible to see for his- or herself that Jesus says *nothing* about homosexuality. Even Saul tempers his words,[70] although Christian exegesis has it that he opposed homosexual men and women and denied them a place in heaven.[71] This denial of a place in heaven has no foundation in scripture.[72]

While contemporary Christians are busy homogenizing, transmogrifying a mortal being into a god that is blemishless and without mortal characteristics, they are in fact subtracting from the very majesty of human condition. This is because Christians are adverse to sex. Sex has been predetermined for the contemporary mind to be evil, based on the erroneous legend of sex being the fruit of the fall (or at least the punishment for the fall) of the "first parents"—the allegorical/mythical "Adam" and "Eve."[73] If human sexuality is accepted as good, the celibate life style and creed of the ancient fathers against sex loses its patina and pales into the distortion of lies that it is. As it tarnishes, the divine is replaced with the corporal, and all people—regardless of their sexual proclivity—must be treated as equals.

Cedar Falls, Iowa
Feast of the Circumcision, 1988

NOTES

[1]Thomas Muentzer was born, probably, in 1488. A Saxon, like Luther, he came from an economically respected house, and in 1506 entered the University at Leipzig. From there he transferred to Frankfurt and ultimately to Mainz, not out of any quest for greater learning, but because he was totally undisciplined. Erratic, he became a priest with no set theological values. He became minister to a small town in eastern Saxony (Zwickau) on the recommendation of Martin Luther. He was forced out of that community because of his radical preaching; this was repeated when he was expelled from Prague. Everywhere he preached about there being an "elect" (Bund), and got into heated war of letters with Martin Luther. When the Roman Catholic chapel at Allstedt was torched, Muentzer's days were numbered. He fled the city in August 1524. Luther turned on him and published his Letter to the Rulers of Saxony Concerning the Rebellious Spirit—in which he insisted that Satan had established a "nest" at Allstedt. Shortly thereafter the peasants discontent broke out into open civil war. When the Peasants' War erupted, Muentzer justified their violence as their "right" against the godless. When the peasants were defeated, Muentzer's fate was sealed. See: M. M. Smirin, Die Volksreformation des Thomas Muentzer und der grosse Bauernkreig (Berlin, 1952) and, Carl Hinrichs, Luther und Muentzer: ihre Auseinandersetzung ueber Obrigkeit und Widerstandsrecht (Berling, 1952), Muentzer's first theological pronouncement was the "Prague Manifesto," published in the fall of 1521, in Otto H. Brandt, Thomas Muentzer (Jena, 1933), pp. 59-62; his troubles are acknowledged at Allstedt in Brandt, Thomas Muentzer, pp. 72-73; and, his endorsement of the Peasants' War in Brandt, Thomas Muentzer, pp. 77-78.

[2]The "blasphemy" of Muentzer is found also in the documents contained in Brandt, Thomas Muentzer, p. 79. Christians attacking Christians based on their interpretation of their bible is well illustrated; for the "evangelicals" (Luther and Calvin) against the "anabaptists" (Muenster and others), see Thielman J. von Braght, The Bloody Theatre or Martyrs' Mirror (Scottdale, 1951).

[3]Nikos Kazantzakis, The Last Temptation of Christ; trans. from the Greek by P. A. Bien (New York: Simon and Schuster; A Touchstone Book, 1960).

[4]John Leo, "A Holy Furor," 132.7 Time (15 August 1988), pp. 34-36.

[5]Glenda M. Locke, "Council targets movie," Mesquite [Texas] News 107. 37 (21 September 1988), pp. 1A, 3A.

[6]Ibid.

[7]Ibid., p. 3A.

[8]*Ibid.* The hypocrisy surrounding the evangelical fanaticism was carried to a new low by Dallas City Council member Al Lipscomb. Al Lipscomb is always seeking new publicity. Once he even recorded a "rap" record.

On Thursday, 1 September 1988, Lipscomb told startled reporters that he intended to *force* his fellow councilmembers to take a public stand on *The Last Temptation of Christ*—and ban the movie. Ignoring his Jewish, Islamic and other non-Christian constituents, Lipscomb not only complained that it offended God, but was "blasphemous depiction of Jesus Christ, our Lord and Savior," and then went on to detail how the movie offended and hurt "the *infant Jesus*"—as if his god had never matured.

Dallas is the last city in the USA that has a censorship board. When it did not censor the movie, evangelical extremists declared a "holy war," with Beth Averitt complaining that "This movie does not fit the [evangelical-fundamentalist Christian] community standard." See: James Ragland, "Lips-

Al Lipscomb

comb plans to force vote on film: He will reintroduce council resolution to condemn 'Temptation'," *The Dallas* [Texas] *Morning News* (2 September 1988), p. 34A. See also: Jim Jones, "Evangelicals issue call to picket 'Last Temptation of Christ'," *Fort Worth* [Texas] *Star-Telegram* (31 August 1988), sec. 1, p. 1, part 2. James Ragland and Ed Housewright, "Council condemns film on Jesus," *The Dallas* [Texas] *Morning News* (25 August 1988), pp. 33A, 40A. Molly Ivins, " 'Last Temptation' just too tempting for Christian censors," *Dallas* [Texas] *Times-Herald* (14 August 1988), p. 21A. Diane Winston, "Christians condemn Jesus film: 'Temptation' sparks peaceful picketing," *Dallas* [Texas] *Times-Herald* (13 August 1988), pp. 1A, 11A.

[9]Glenda M. Locke, "Council targets movie," *Mesquite* [Texas] *News* 107.37 (21 September 1988), p. 3A. On the venalty of the City of Mesquite's fascist government, see my: *Democracy Dies In Dallas: Cops, Lies & Videotapes* (Garland, TX: Tangelwuld, 1990), index.

[10]Dan Malone, "Ex-chairman of Tarrant GOP calls foes on film vote 'satanic'," *The Dallas* [Texas] *Morning News* (25 August 1988), p. 40A.

[11]Diane Winston, "Texas Christians join film battle: Some say studios want dispute on 'Last Temptation of Jesus'," *Dallas* [Texas] *Times-Herald* (31 July 1988) pp. 1B, 6B.

[12]Darrell Dunn, " 'Temptation gathers yet another rally," *Dallas* [Texas] *Times Herald* (21 August 1988), sec. B, pp. 1, 7.

[13]Associated Press, "Thousands protest on eve of film's release," in *Fort Worth* [Texas] *Star-Telegram* (12 August 1988), sec. 1, p. 6.

[14]Louis Moore, "New movie rekindles old debate about Jesus," *Fort Worth* [Texas] *Star-Telegram* (10 August 1988), sec. 1, p. 19. Editorial, "Last temptation of Lipscomb," *Dallas* [Texas] *Times Herald* (20 August 1988), sec. A, p. 18. Leslie Hicks, "Video outlets may decide not to stock movie," *Fort Worth* [Texas] *Star-Telegram* (13 August 1988), sec. 1, pp. 1, 13: and in the same issue: Holly Hanson, " 'Last Temptation,' Scorsese's movie opens amid protests, long lines," *ibid.*, pp. 1, 12. Christian lawyers came out against it, as well, with the "reverend" Wayne House, who is also a professor at Dallas Theological Seminary, declaring, as if he were in the Hitler's Youth congress, piling faggots around "unacceptable" books and films, "I think they ought to burn it." Nazi thinking went even further with the "reverend" Norton Richardson, a bitter opponent of the First Amendment, who called the movie, "a blasphemous film projecting Jesus as a weakling and immoral. This isn't a question of First Amendment rights; it's about an erroneous portrayal of Jesus." See: Diane Winston, "Texas Christians join in film battle; Some say studios want dispute on 'Last Temptation of Jesus [sic]," *Dallas* [Texas] *Times Herald* (31 July 1988), sec. B, pp. 1, 6. Ten Mesquite, Texas, cops vowed they'd "burn down the houses" of any citizen that would have "such pornography," for "we believe more in Jesus Christ than the Constitution."

[15]Associated Press, "Film theft delays 'Last Temptation,' showing," *Dallas* [Texas] *Times Herald* (27 August 1988), sec. A, p. 19. Fascists came out of the woodwork, demanding that stronger measures were used to water down the First Amendment of the U. S. Constitution: the pyres of Adolf Hitler and the book burning in Communist China and Stalinist Russia seemed the only answer, one that seemed worthy to some. For popular reaction against the film, with overt totalitarian overtones, see Angie Reese, " 'Last Temptation' is only the beginning," *Mesquite* [Texas] *News* (4 September 1988), sec. A, p. 4. For a further development of this topic and the nefarious mentality of Mesquite evangelicals/fundamentalists, see my: *Censorship in the U.S.A,* forthcoming. It should be noted that these "Christians," as is typical with members of the conservative wing of fundamentalism, is that are quite selective about what scripture (bible) they read or believe in. Few acknowledge Hebrews 4:15: Jesus was "tempted in all things as we are" (*New American Standard Bible*).

[16]Nikos Kazantzakis, *The Last Temptation of Christ*, pp. 1, 4.

[17]J. Michael Clark, *A Defiant Celebration* (Garland, TX: Tangelwuld, 1990). See also my: *Sex, Woman & Religion* (Dallas, TX: Monument Press, 1985).

[18]Outside of the gospels of Mark, Matthew, Luke and John, there is no historical record, written by contemporaries, that Jesus ever existed. "Jesus" is a Greek formed word (Ἰησους) of the Hebrew *Joshua*, which literally means "JHVH [Jehovah] saves." This was not the infant son of Joseph the Carpenter and Mary the espoused when he was first born. "God," literally, changed it (Matt. 1:21; cp. Luke 1:31). Christian apologists, who attempt to link ancient writers as authorities who recognized and accepted the personhood of Jesus, err. Cornelius Tacitus (c. 55-120), merely mentions in his *Annals* XV:44, that Christians were persecuted by Nero. There is no affirmation of the manhood/divinity of a son of a carpenter in Israel. Most of the ancient Christians were, in fact, reformed Jews, and the Christ they cited was the Old Testament Joshua who had initiated the rite of circumcision to set their men apart from the uncircumcised Romans and other gentiles. See: J. M. Robertson, *Pagan Christs* (New Hyde Park, NY: University Books, 1967). All aspects of the "Jesus" fixation can be traced back to Babylonian myths and Sacaean mysteries and rituals.

[19]The goodness of the kiss (*osculum pacis*) is first mentioned by Justin Martyr in the second century CE, who elaborated upon references to it found in Rom. 16:16, 1 Pet. 5, 14). See: H. Thurston, *Catholic Encyclopedia*, 8 (1910), pp. 663-665. and F. Cabrol, "Basier," in *Dictionnaire d'Archeologie Chretienne et de Liturgie* 2 (1910), cols. 117-130.

[20]Luke 7.38: Φαρισαιον κομισασα αλαβαστρον μυρου και στασα οπισω παρα τους ποδας αυτου κλαιουσα ηρξατο βρεχειν τους ποδας αυτος τοις δακρυσι και ταις θριξι της κεφαλης αυτης εξεμαξε και κατεφιλει τους ποδας ···

[21]Luke 15:20: και αναστας ηλθε προς τον πατερα εαυτον· ετι δε αυτου μακραν απεχοντος ειδεν αυτον ο πεπηρ αυτον και εσπλαγχνισθη· και δραμων επεπεσεν επι τον τραχηλον αυτου και κατεφιλησεν αυτυ·

[22]Matt. 26:49: και κατεφιλησεν αυτον.

[23]Mark 14:45: Ραββι και κατεφιλησεν αυτον.

[24]Luke 22:47: Επι αυτου λαλουντος ιδουοχλος και ο λεγομενος Ιουδας εις των δωδεκα προηρχετο αυτων·

[25]John 18:10f.

[26]Matt. 26:49; notice, in the following line, Jesus refers to Judas as his friend, not his betrayer: εταιρος, meaning "comrad" or "equal." This is an indication that the entire plot of the arrest had been prearranged with Jesus' full knowledge and consent. This being the case would give credence to the frequently speculated theory that Jesus and his group wanted to become a part of the mystery cults of birth-death-resurrection, as was popular in Egypt (Osiris) and throughout the growing Roman world (Mithra). He does not call Judas his com-

panion (or "pal"), which would be φιλος. Numerous other references supports arguments that the "betrayal" and "crucifixion" were contrived. See my forthcoming: *Jesus Christ?*

[27]Luke 7:37-38.

[28]Luke 7:45: φιλημα μοι ουκ εδωκας αυτη δε αφ ης εισηλθον ου διελιπε καταφιλουσα.

[29]Acts 20:37: ικανος δε εγενετο κλαυθμος παντων- και επιπεσοντες επι τον τραχηλον του Παυλου κατεφιλουν αυτον.

[30]Gen. 29:13, 31:28, 55 and 45:15; Ps. 2:12; Ruth 1:9, 14.

[31]It was neither *neshiqah* nor φιλημα

[32]ακολουθεω; cp. Matt. 8:10, 19 and 9:9; Mark 10:21, 28; Luke 9:23.

[33]Cp. Rom. 16:16; I Cor. 16:16; 2 Cor. 13:12; 1 Thess. 5:26; I Pet. 5:14.

[34]Matt. 26:10; Mark 14:6, details Jesus' insight behind acts, from the day he was anointed by Mary, to his meeting with Judas in the garden: Matt. 26:50.

[35]Luke 7:44-46.

[36]αγιον πνευμα. The exchange of kisses in the early Christian community is discussed in my *Martyrdom of Women: A Study of Death Psychology in the Early Christian Church to 301 CE* (Garland, TX: Tangelwuld Press, 1985), pp. 45-68. See also mv: *The Kiss As A Spiritual Bond* (Toronoto: Theological Inquiry Press, 1980). This remained a facet in medieval vassalage: *"Primum hominia fecerunt ita: comes requisivit si inteare vellet homo suus fieri, et ille respondit: 'volo' et junctis manibus, amplexatus a manibus comitis, osculo confederati sunt."* in Galbert of Burges, *Histoire du meurte de Charles le Bon, comte de Flandre*, c. 56 (ed. Henri Pirenne; Paris, 1891), p. 89. The *osculum* was equal to the *immixtio manuum*, intended to impress the spectators and give a physical sign to a mental bonding. By the late Middle Ages, especially in France, this carried the concept of *hommage de bouche et de mains*, and a vassal was described as *homme de bouche et de mains*. For reference, see the invaluable *Monumenta Germaniae Historica, Scriptores* II:141. Cp. *Recogniciones feodorum in Aquitainia* (1273-75), no. 11, in C. Bemont, *Recueil d'actes relatifs a l'administration des rois d'Angleterre en Guyenne au XIIIe siecle* (Paris, 1914), p. 15.

[37]Andre Haynal, Miklos Molnar and Gerard de Puymege, *Le fanatisme: ses racines; Une essai historique et psychanalytique* (Paris: Editions Stock, 1980), chap. 2. Fred H. Johnson, *The Anatomy of Hallucinations* (Chicago: Nelson-Hall,

1978), pp. 158-166. Albert Schwitzer, *The Psychiatric Study of Jesus: Exposition and Criticism* (Boston: Beacon Press, 1948). While there are many studies today which argue, most convincingly, that Jesus was mentally ill, this was not an uncommon assumption even in the days Jesus allegedly walked on the earth. His own disciples questioned his sanity, believing that Jesus was "beside himself": και ακουσαντες οι παρ αυτου εξηθον κρατησαι αυτον· ελεγον γαρ οτι Εξεστη, Mark 3: 21, being a subtle way of saying "mad," (as it's commonly translated in the Douay and Rheims editions, and many English Protestant editions. See also: William Houston Clark, *The Psychology of Religion; An Introduction to Religious Experience and Behavior* (New York: Macmillan, 1967), p. 343; Vann Spruiell, "Narcissistic Transformations in Adolescence," *International Journal of Psychoanalytic Psychotherapy* 4 (1975), pp. 530-531.

[38] Luke 4:13: και λεγει αυτοις 'Ουκ οιδατε την παραβολην ταυτην.

[39] Cf. Fred H. Johnson, *The Anatomy of Hallucinations*, pp. 98, 110, 147-152. Religion has for too long equated human sexuality with sin; this absurd concept has caused many psychological problems, and has initiated, spread, and intensified sexual fantasies and corelative problems, as demonstrated by the fictional character Ethan Brand in Hawthorne's wonderful fiction, and studied by Alfred Kinsey. See: Alfred C. Kinsey, *Sexual Behavior in the Human Male* (Philadelphia: W. B. Saunders, 1948). Those who elect to chain themselves to unnatural celibacy or live lives of conspicuous piety and chastity, in nearly every case, have mental problems. See: James H. Leuba, *The Psychology of Religious Mysticism* (New York: Harcourt, Brace & Co., 1925), chaps. 4, 7; with a detailed discussion on the eroticism of fantasies plaguing the unnaturally celibate on pages 145-146.

[40] The devil is an allusion towards fecundity and sexuality. In all ancient representations of this mythical/fantasy being, its presented with horns: phallic in nature and purpose. The Old Testament Devil is hard to separate from the Old Testament god Yahweh, since it's Yahweh who is evil, shows no mercy, and contradicts righteousness: Judges 2:1, where Yahweh upbraids the Jews for showing mercy; 2 Sam 17:14, where Yahweh purposefully leads Absalom into "sin"; Isaiah 6:9-11, where destruction is a special joy! Today Christians paint the Devil red—but red is also the color painted on the Evil One outside the pagan temple of Marduk. The occasional instances of a Black Devil is in retaliation for Seth and the consumption of pork. The Devil is also presented as Lilith—the allegorial second wife of the fictional character "Adam" in the "Creation Narrative." All these symbols and representations can be seen in the art and iconography of India, Egypt and Mesopotamia. Cp. Luke 4:25-26, 33, 38-41.

[41] Luke 4:40-42.

[42] Luke 4:40: Δυνοντος δε του ηλιου παντες οσοι ειχον ασθενουντας νοσοις ποικιλαις ηγαγον αυτους προς αυτον ο δε ενι εκαςτω αυτων τας χειρας επιθεις εθεραπευσεν αυτους.

[43]Matt. 17:1; Mark 5:37, 9:2; Luke 8:51, 9:54; Acts 1:13, 3:1, 3. John was the most favored, as noted in John 13:25, which even Peter admitted (John 21:20).

[44]Και τουτο ειπων λεγει αυτω Ακολουθει μοι· επιστραφεις ο Πετρος βλεπει τον μαθητην ον ηγαπα ο Ιησους ακολουθουντα ος και ανεπεσεν τω δειπνω επι το στηθος αυτου και ειπε.

[45]Morton Smith, The Secret Gospel: The Discovery & Interpretation of the Secret Gospel According to Mark (London: Dawn Horse Press, 1974), pp. 14-16ff. Compare this youth to the one in the official gospel of Mark 14:51-52 and John 11:13.

[46]John 11:3-5, 11, 15-16.

[47]In the Hebrew the word is also interchangeable for an "anointed" leader (see. Daniel 9:25-26). In the Greek at the time of the alleged Christ, it was understood to mean "preceeding one" (John 1:41 and 4:25) which could have been applied to John the Baptist. The Black Mass was a popular Roman initiation rite for young men. Sometimes it was used to feast the dead, as recorded by Dio Cassius LXVII:9-10; a translation is given in my Woman in the Age of Christian Martyrs (Mesquite, TX: IHP, 1982), pp. 42-44, and summarized with analysis in my Martyrdom of Women, pp. 72-74. With the ascent of the Christian church, the Black Mass was outlawed as being a celebration of evil and the Mass for the Devil—which it never was.

[48]Michael Baigent, Richard Leigh and Henry Lincoln, Holy Blood, Holy Grail (New York: Dell, 1982, 1983), pp. 339-340, 372-374.

[49]John 11:36: ελεγον ουν οι Ιουδαιοι Ιδε πως εφιλει αυτον. Note that this love is not αγαπαω—a spiritual love, nor a theological (θελω) love. It's more intense and personal. The debate on John/Lazarus continues, especially in review of the common concensus that Jesus "loved" him. See: W. H. Brownless' interesting article, "Whence the Gospel According to John," in James H. Charlesworth (ed.), John and Qumran (London: Geoffrey Chapman Publishers, 1972), p. 192. See also: Donovan Joyce, The Jesus Scroll (London: Sphere, 1975), p. 22.

[50]See my. Born Again: the Pagan Antecedents to a Christian Concept (Toronto: Theological Inquiry Press, 1981).

[51]Jewish law demanded all men marry. Celibacy was unheard of. Cf. William E. Phipps, Was Jesus Married? The Distortion of Sexuality in the Christian Tradition (New York: University Press of America, 1970, 1986). see also his: Sexuality of Jesus (New York: University Press of America, 1973).

[52]John 12:1-3.

93

[53] Luke 10:38-42; cp. John 11:21.

[54] Leviticus 17-26; nudity is damned throughout chapter 18. and 20:19, See also my: *Woman in Ancient Israel Under the Torah & the Talmud* (Mesquite, TX: IHP, 1982).

[55] Mark 14:51-52: Και οεαοισκος τις συνηκολουθει αυτω περιβεβλημενος συνδονα επι γυμνου- και κρατουσιν αυτον- ο δε καταληπων την συνδονα γυμνος εφυγε.

[56] Mark 14:51, Matt. 27:59, and Luke 23:53.

[57] John 19:40.

[58] Gen. 41:42, Ex. 24:4, 26:1, 31 and 36.

[59] Rev. 18:16, 19:18 and 14.

[60] It must be remembered that the gospels were composed/written after 64-74 CE, when Judaism ceased to be a organized, social, political and military force, and they were written for a Greco-Roman audience; therefore the distinctions could not be subtle, and if Jesus was truly "a King" (Mark 15:2, 12), he would have to be buried in cloth fitting his station. Also, if Jesus were to become acceptable, he could not be tainted with the image of a common criminal—even if his execution was that of a common criminal. Jesus was condemned by the Sanhedrin—the Council of Jewish Elders—who brought him to Pilate. Pilate only goes along with their wishes in an effort to keep peace, according to the gospels. This in itself is a lie, for Judaic law prohibited the Sanhedrin from meeting during Passover—the time period during which Jesus was arrested, tried, and allegedly executed. Second, while the gospels claim that the Sanhedrin was forbidden to pass a death sentence, history shows otherwise: they could have condemned Jesus to death by stoning. None of the New Testament accounts of the arrest, trial, and alleged execution fit with history or fact. See: H. Cohn: *Trial and Death of Jesus* (New York: KATV, 1971), pp. 166ff. An ex-attorney general of Israel, and member of the Supreme Court, Hiram Cohn is eminently suited to the task of analyzing the situation; he is a lecturer on historical law.

[61] The contemporary bible is not the original bible. Many of the letters (*epistles*) and gospels (now considered spurious or false) were thrown out of the official canon. The exclusion of books based on variant interpretations continued until 1672, when the Eastern Church at the Synod of Jerusalem, rejected all but four of the Septuagint canon: keeping only the books of Tobias, Judith, Ecclesiasticus, and Wisdom. Protestants excluded the Apocrypha at the time of the Reformation in the sixteenth century. The Christian βιβλια—or bible—was formalized at Rome in 328 CE. Jerome further defined it, excluding the Deuterocanonical books from the Christian corpus.

[62] John 12:10.

[63] John 11:4.

[64] John 11:11.

[65] Morton Smith, *Jesus the Magician* (New York: Harper & Row, 1978), p. 81f. In early Christianity the Antichrist is also presented as a miracle worker: the belief was that Jesus was only a more powerful miracle worker. John 11:16 gives an account how Thomas wants to go with Jesus so that he, too, "can die" with him—common elements in the mystery cult of resurrection.

[66] John 11:36.

[67] John 13:23-26.

[68] Hugh J. Schonfield, *The Passover Plot: New Light on the History of Jesus* (New York: Bernard Geis Associates; distributed by Random House, 1965), 134f.

[69] Fundamentalists take literal words and still distort them: see my *Unholy Rollers: Televangelism & the Selling of Jesus* (Arlington, TX: Liberal Arts Press, 1986), my *Robertson: The Pulpit and the Power: Pat's Putsche for the Presidency* (Austin, TX: AAP, 1989); and my: *Heaven's Hustler: the Fall & Rise of Jimmy Swaggart* (Dallas, TX: Monument Press, 1988).

[70] See my: *Gomorrah & the Rise of Homophobia* (Las Colinas, TX: The Liberal Press, 1985).

[71] This is based on a misreading of Romans 1:27.

[72] See my: *City of Sodom: Homosexuality in Western Religious Thought to 630 CE* (Dallas, TX: Monument Press, 1985).

[73] See my: *Sex, Woman & Religion* (Dallas, TX: Monument Press, 1984); my *Woman in Ancient Israel Under the Torah & the Talmud ; with a Critical Commentary on Genesis 1-3* (Mesquite, TX: IHP, 1963), and, my *Vows, Virgins, Oaths & Orgies* (Arlington, TX: Liberal Arts Press, 1989).

95

INDEX

GLOSSARY

bible   Originally, it was the name of a Phoenician city (*Byblos*) from which papyrus was exported (today the city is known as Jubayl or Jebeil; the Christian bible refers to it as Gebal [Eze. 27:9]). It's an ancient seaport on the coast of Lebanon, and probably the oldest continuously inhabited town in the world. It plays a role in the history of ancient civilizations, including the Amorites (literally "mountaineers", cf. Gen. 10.16, 14.7, 13ff), Hyksos, Phoenicians, Greeks and Romans as well as throughout the medieval periods (the crusaders captured it in 1103 and called it Gibelet, but lost it to the Islamic leader Saladin in 1189). It's 17 miles to the north of Beirut and south of Tripoli.

It's significance and prominence was assured since the days of the Myceneans because of its papyrus (which the Greeks called *byblos*, or "book"), and because the goddess Biblis conducted a part of her search for her brother Caunus (she loved him and wanted him for her husband and lover, but he refused her advances), and was ultimately transformed into a weeping fountain. Her cult was centered in Asia Minor and became a popular romantic tale and ritual in the Hellenistic age, with such writers as Ovid, furthering her legend.

Her cult and the subsequent history of the city extended to the Neolithic and Bronze Ages, and because of the papyrus commerce, melted into the Egyptian culture. From Egypt the cult and especially the worship of the book (or any written word, since literacy was marginal, and a writer was of the priestly class) spread to and impregnated the ancient Hebrews and ultimately the Christians who believed that any written statement detailing god (later reserved exclusively for the gods of the Old and New Testaments) was special and holy.

The growth of the worship of the female was at a high point during the twelfth dynasty in Egypt when the city again became a dependency, and its chief goddess, *Baalat* (literally "the Lady") was admitted into the Egyptian pantheon. In the twelfth century BCE, after the collapse of the New Egyptian empire Byblos became the foremost πολις (city-state) in Phoenicia. See. Pierre Montet, *Byblos et l' Egypte* (Paris: P. Geuthner, 1928), and Maurice Dunand, *Fouilles de Byblos* (Paris: P. Geuthner, 1937), vols. 1-3. Also see Arthur Frederick Ide, *The Writing of the Bible* (Quebec: Theology, 1978).

born again A term originally used to signify (or separate) an individual who is born into one nation but assumes the national status and liberties/obligations of another. In Jewish circles it was commonly understood to mean a Jew who also was a Roman citizen, as in the case of Saul of Tarsus: Τι μελλεις ποιεω ο γαρ ανθρωπος ουτος Ρωμαιος εστι προσελθων δε ο χιλιαρχης ειπεν αυτω Λεγε μοι συ Ρωμαιος ει ο δε εφη Ναι απεκριθη δε ο χιλιαρχος Εγω πολλου κεφαλαιου την πολιτειαν ταυτην εκτησεμην (Acts 22:27-78). This "adoption" or rebirth could be washed away with a water baptism (cf. John 1:26 and 1 John 5:6).

Pharisee   Litterally "separated." It was a word used to set a person aside from mainstream Jewish civilization. The Pharisee belonged to a school or party that was noted for strict or formal observance of rites and ceremonies of the written law, and for insistence on the validity of the traditions of the elders. The Pharisee believed in the immortality of the soul, the resurrection of the the physical body after death and decay, future retribution (hell) or reward (heaven), and the coming of a prophecied Messiah. The majority of first century Christians were Pharisical Jews.

Resurrection   Originally this word mean "to rise" or "surge forward"—from an inferior state into a superior state (from poverty to wealth, from slave to free, from bad to good health, from decay to rejuvenation, from disuse to use). With the rise of numerous mystery religions in the Middle East, it took on the meaning of "rising from the dead" to live either on earth or in a spiritual place of unearthly qualities—either in the old repurified body, or a new body—or, in some cases, as a ghost.

Sadducee   Originating from the name of the high priest Zadok who lived during the reign of David, it was applied to members of a party or sect of Jews from the second century BCE to the end of the first century CE. The majority were priestly aristocracy who opposed, both politically and doctrinally, the Pharisees for their strictness. Sadducees gave a more liberal interpretation pf the law. They reject other parts of the Jewish scriptures and rabbinic tradition. They deny the resurrection of the body, personal immortality, retribution in the future (hell) or an existence with the angels (heaven), the existence of angels, demons, devils, saints and spirits. Sadducees believed in materialism and self-fulfillment. They were either indifferent to religion or atheists.

Sanhedrin   Literally: a "council." It was the supreme council and tribunal of the ancient Hebrew nation, consisting of 70-72 members. It had jurisdiction over religious matters and important civil and criminal cases. It created several provincial councils that had 23 members and jurisdiction over minor civil and criminal cases.

Compiled by the Editor